WEB

OF

DARKNESS

WEB

OF

DARKNESS

by
Sean Sellers

Victory House, Inc.
Tulsa, Oklahoma

Unless otherwise indicated, all Scripture quotations are taken from the *King James Version* of the Bible.

Table of Contents

There shall not be found among you any one that maketh his son or his daughter to pass through the fire, or that useth divination, or an observer of times, or an enchanter, or a witch, Or a charmer, or a consulter with familiar spirits, or a wizard, or a necromancer. For all that do these things are an abomination unto the Lord; and because of these abominations the Lord thy God doth drive them out from before thee.

(Deuteronomy 18:10-12)

Foreword

Satan — the origin of death, disease, and despair, all that is negative in the universe. Why, then, do so many teens fall prey to his demonic deception? What are they searching for, and how do they find it as servants of Satan?

These are only a few of the questions that Americans ask in confusion. As headlines continue to herald the onslaught of satanic schemes, one must continue to wonder where our society has erred. How did we fail to reach teenagers before satanism enticed them?

There are as many answers as there are teen satanists. Some young men and women choose evil because of low self-esteem. Others suffered such terrible abuse that Satan's promise of revenge captures them. Still others believe Satan will provide all their needs, including love, power, and possessions.

We can help deceived satanists escape this evil snare. We can prevent other troubled teens from choosing evil over good, hell over heaven, and Satan over God. Knowledge and information are our most formidable weapons to defeat Satan. In *Web of Darkness,* Sean Sellers imparts both.

I've known about Sean Sellers since the day his story became national news. Who could have ignored the story of a young man, charged with the murder of his parents and a convenience store clerk and who claimed that Satan directed his actions? I remember wondering what was going to happen to this rebellious teen. Little did I know then that several years later I would talk to Sean, live from death row at the Oklahoma State Penitentiary, on my national talk show, TALK-BACK.

The Sean I heard was different than the teen who murdered his parents in cold blood. He was now a vocal Christian. Though he faced death for first-degree murder, Sean spoke with the calm assurance of one who has dealt with reasons for his crimes, and what he does with his life now.

The show was called "The Devil and Death Row." My goal was to convince teens who dabbled in devil worship that Satan's lies would lead them to a hellish fate. Sean's terrifying tale of mayhem and murder chilled listeners and drew troubled teens to the phones. He reached teens on their own level and graphically showed them the devil's deception.

As I listened to Sean deal gently and firmly with rebellious teen callers, I knew God had changed his life. I believe that change is evident in *Web of Darkness.*

Web of Darkness is a book for adults who need to wake up and learn how Satan snares society. It's a book for teens who are so caught up in their satanic sacrifices and ghoulish games that they can't see the demonic destruction before them. Most important, it's a book for those who want to fight against Satan's schemes. Sean Sellers deserves admiration and respect, not for his past crimes, but for his current commitment to reaching teens.

It's easy to dismiss the ills of our society today, to bury our heads and hope the dangerous decline into satanism simply goes away. It won't! I know it, and Sean knows it! The greatest weapon Satan has in society is silence. Sean Sellers fights that silence from death row. We must join his fight for the sake of our children.

— Bob Larson

Preface

Today more and more people are getting involved in occultism and various satanic deceptions. Some pattern their life-styles after ideals which have become perverted and corrupted; others have become involved with occult games, like the Ouija Board, Tarot cards, and crystals. Most people, especially teenagers, seem to think these things are harmless, and even worse, many of the games are thought of as being cool and quite neat. The fact is, they are neither. All these things are quite dangerous satanic deceptions.

Many hard and dreadful experiences have taught me that you cannot play games with the devil; *he simply does not play games.* (You cannot play games with God either). Many people unwittingly fill their lives with ideals and actions based on occult beliefs from ancient paganism, and some are playing around with "toys" or "games" that were used in the past by witches and sorcerers as tools to the black arts. Today these products are still used as tools by trained occultists. People who are involved in active satanism know full well the power that such simple "games" as the Ouija Board possess.

The concept behind each of these so-called games is focused on discovering that which is unknown through the petitioning of spiritual powers. In the realm of the occult this is known as "consulting an oracle" (a demon).

Whether a participant realizes it or not, such involvement opens the door to satanic deception and demonic control.

Each of the above ideals, life-styles, and games lead the individual who uses them to make a choice against God and to adhere to demonic activity. Many times this choice is made unknowingly.

Drugs and some music can destroy the mind and alter a person's belief patterns. Perverted sex always causes problems, with AIDS being one of the least of today's sex-related problems.

In the same way that the recreational use of drugs often leads people into addiction, a lot of teenagers who become involved and trapped in satanism begin by playing around with one of these "games." The "game" may be purchased by them or played on a dare. A person or group may begin to play casually or experiment with one of the "games" just for kicks, or, on Halloween, to enter into the spirit of the season.

Soon the group plays every week. Then it becomes an obsession with a few of them, and they play every night, or one may play alone.

The next step involves *worship*. Before one even realizes completely the changes that are taking place in his attitudes, he finds himself worshiping Satan; before long, he is cutting himself, drinking blood, doing drugs, and sooner or later, he simply burns out.

In drug abuse, no one starts out by saying, "I'm going to be a crack addict," or "I'm going to be a heroin freak." It begins with smoking a joint, taking a pill, smoking a rock, and before the changes are even realized, the most important thing becomes getting the next fix.

In the same way, satanism leads to nowhere. Fear, pain, and loneliness are the inevitable results of the occult, and all the perverted ideals and so-called occult games are doorways into the pathway to nowhere.

This book is written to address these problems and to educate those who have questions about them. As you read, may you become enlightened.

To Those Who Are Involved in Occultism

The things in this book are true. I have written based on my own experiences and studies, and the experiences of others who have come through these same problems. When I was only a dabbler, playing unknowingly with some of the "games" mentioned herein, I scoffed and laughed at those who felt compelled to warn me of the so-called dangers.

People seem to take great joy in ridiculing things with which they cannot agree. Perhaps it is because if those things are right or true, then something in the way we have chosen to live is wrong. Instead of acknowledging the wrong it becomes more convenient to disregard the truth. When we are young we are often arrogant, and foolish, but in time we must all grow up.

There is a spiritual world far more real than our physical world. Our physical senses reveal to us only a fragment of reality. Please read the following pages slowly. I am sure there will be many who will scoff and ridicule these observations even as I once did. I have seen those foolish seeds of ridicule planted in others' lives as well as my own. And I have watched as they grew into something that consumed those lives. I pray that your time to grow up is now.

— Sean Sellers —

PART I

My Personal Story

Therefore if any man be in Christ, he is a new creature: old things are passed away; behold, all things are become new.

(2 Corinthians 5:17)

1
New Life on Death Row

"Aren't you afraid?" Cheryl, a girl in my art class, asked, holding her paint brush poised to the canvas. Her cute face was framed by brown hair. This petite young woman was a talented artist. I liked her, but I could not resist trying to shock her.

"Afraid? Babe, I *am* what people fear," I smiled wickedly.

She blinked. "I mean about going to hell," she said questioningly, still not understanding the person she had been painting next to in high school art class for six months. The person she had thought was pretty cool — weird, but cool! — was a practicing satanist!

"Nah, I have a round-trip ticket so I'm not worried about hell." Cheryl backed up a couple of steps.

"Cheryl," I said grinning, "it's still me — Sean! You've known me all year. I've been a satanist for nearly two years. I haven't changed overnight or anything."

She shook her head. "How can anyone be a satanist? I mean, why do you *want* to worship the devil?"

If you only knew, I thought. "Look around you. What do you think about this little world we live in?"

"It's not so bad," she said.

"Girl — you're fried! Just check it out. Look around you. You've got dweebs like that drip over there." I gestured toward a kid who was asleep on his drawing table. (I had smoked a joint with him before class.) "Do you really think he enjoys life? He's worn the same pants to school for three days. And check out Miss Priss over there, primping in front of the mirror. That's right, Sweetie, I'm talking about you. Oh, by the way, you missed hair number 99," I smirked. The girl tried to ignore me.

I turned back to Cheryl. "Have you ever seen her wear anything twice? The only thing she comes in here with that we've seen before is that suitcase of a purse she carries her makeup in."

"Okay, so maybe life's not so fair, but — "

"I'm not talking about fair, Doll. No one ever promised us that life would be fair. What I'm talking about is *God.* "

"What do you mean?" she asked.

I leaned against the counter where the paints were kept. "You know the crowd Amy hangs out with? What's that on top of her books? A Bible, right? She's a Christian and, personally, she's one of the most stuck-up 'cherries' I know.

"Oh, God has been good to her alright. She's probably got a credit card with her name on it. If I were her, I'd be a Christian too. But what the hell has your precious God ever done for me? Everything I've got I had to work for. Damn hard too.

"You see that pickup I drive? Yeah, it's a '73 Ford, white with a green door, dented like crazy. Well, it may not be much, but it's mine. I worked for it. My parents didn't help me."

"So?" Cheryl shrugged.

"So, what I'm saying is we live in America. We work for what we get. And if your God really cares, He has a strange way of showing it. Do unto others as you would have them do unto you — and get walked on, because this world is really messed up. I say do unto others as they do unto you. Let me ask you something. If someone came up and slapped you, would you hit them back?"

"Probably."

"See? I thought Christians were supposed to turn the other cheek."

"I didn't say I was a Christian," Cheryl argued.

"You're not a Christian?" I asked.

"Well, I don't know — "

"You're living by an ideal of satanism. Do you know where 'Do unto others as they do unto you' comes from? THE SATANIC BIBLE. So you're living an ideal of Satan and you think I'm weird because I've got my eyes open?"

I left Cheryl confused.

That night as I got off work, the conversation came up in my mind. I sat in my pickup in the parking lot with the door open, smoking a cigarette. Beside me lay a briefcase and on top of it my knife. I picked up the double-edged boot knife and tossed it on the dash as I opened the briefcase. I sorted through the books on Ninjutsu, astral projection, witchcraft, runes, and picked up a blood-smeared copy of THE SATANIC BIBLE.

Satan represents undefiled wisdom instead of hypocritical self-deceit.

People are so blind, I thought. I tossed my cigarette onto the pavement and sighed. From out of my pocket I took a small vial of blood. Tilting it back and forth, I watched the bubbles snap, leaving specks on the glass until I turned it over, washing it crimson again. I removed the cap and touched my tongue to the top, tasting it. (I had gotten used to its salty-metallic taste.) Then I poured it into my mouth and let the warmth of it cover my teeth. Swallowing it, I thought, "And people think vampires only live in the movies."

I fished in the glove box for some No-Doze and took out the small bottle. I poured the pills out in my hand and swallowed two of them with a white-cross (speed). Closing the glove box, I leaned back and sighed. "Speed. Blood. Satanism. I don't know, Sean. Maybe you are going crazy," I said to myself. "God, I hate this life. How did I get so confused?"

My mind went back to thirteen. Always thirteen. Every time I questioned my life, I always started at thirteen. I was finally a teenager. It seemed like the proverbial unlucky number.

I had been raised on country music and had begun to drift toward rock and roll. On the bus home from school, Boston's "Smoking" would jam from the back seats where we sat, followed by "I Love Rock and Roll" by Joan Jett. MTV was just beginning with videos like "Jack and Diane" by John Cougar and "Words" by Missing Persons.

Beneath the few books I carried home with my football equipment was a notebook filled with Dungeons & Dragons material. I had four primary interests: I played football, practiced Ninjutsu, collected comic books, and played D & D.

I was a Dungeon Master and I also played a character. We ran three different campaigns. I DMed in two of them and played my neutral/chaotic fighter in the third. Nobody understood the game as well as I. I read, I studied the manuals. I created new and more intense Dungeon modules. All of my spare time in school was taken up in my study of D & D.

And at home, it was Ninjutsu. The ninjamania craze had yet to hit the U.S., so there was not much material on it to be found. I practiced daily with my cousin, who introduced me to it. He was eighteen and we would go into the yard and spar. When he worked, I practiced *nunchakus, shuriken,* and *bokken.* At night we "played hide and seek." I learned how to walk quietly in leaves and sticks. I learned how to fight.

We moved to Colorado and I continued to study with what had become my hobbies. After a year, I had left football behind and I joined the Civil Air Patrol (CAP). I attended special training schools, became a NEAT (National Emergency Assistance Training) qualified Ranger, graduating with an outstanding cadet merit. A few months later, I was the squadron cadet commander.

I continued to focus on Ninjutsu. I walked out of the movies one night disgusted after watching "Revenge of the Ninja." All the acrobatics and costumes were foolishness. I began to ask myself, "Do I really know what Ninjutsu is all about?" I began to study. I learned about the spiritual focusing of Zen meditation and began disciplining my mind even more.

Nights, I prepared to organize my CAP squadron, worked out, punching out candle flames, and meditated.

On my regular trips to the library, I researched the origins and legends of dragons. The people I played D & D with were getting too cocky. Their characters needed to learn humility, I had decided. So I planned to "bring to life" in the game a powerful dragon from mythology that could only be defeated with a riddle.

Zen had taught me that battles were won in the mind first and didn't always have to be fought physically. I wanted to teach that to those I played with.

The research on dragons led me to the Time/Life series of books on the occult. I began reading about wizards and witches, and I remembered an episode when I was younger in which a baby-sitter had checked out some books on witchcraft and satanism for me. That memory led me to turn my study toward satanism and related subjects.

All day I looked through the card catalog and library shelves. I looked up demons, witches, Salem, witchcraft, evil, Satan, satanism, voodoo, and whatever else I could find. There was something that mysteriously connected all this with my study of Ninjutsu, and I was resolved to find it. There was power in the supernatural world, and I wanted to learn how to harness and use it.

Around the same time I became angry with God and began to hate Him. I had met a girl and had fallen in love with her, regardless of the fact that everyone was telling me I was too young to know what love is. During a phone call one night while my parents were gone for a few days, she told me to get out of her life and leave her alone.

I had met the girl a year before in church. She was my first real kiss. And now I felt dead inside. I decided to kill myself. I went to my bedroom, got my shotgun, and placed it in the middle of the living room floor. With my cleaning kit, I began to take it apart and oil it. As I did so, I started thinking about how everyone would feel about my being gone. I began to miss *me*. And as I placed the number-four shell into the newly oiled chamber and pulled the bolt back, placing the gun barrel to my chin, I said out loud, "What, am I — freaking crazy? What the hell am I doing?"

I put the gun down, called a friend, and asked him to come over. When he walked in, he saw the gun, and after hearing my story, he decided to stay the night. We got drunk.

I had prayed to God that this girl would love me as I loved her. God had failed me. He didn't love me. I hated Him. I wanted nothing to do with God anymore. It was my friends, not God, not my family, who were there when I needed them. I could depend on my friends, no one else — except myself. The year was 1982.

We moved again. Returning to Oklahoma, from Colorado, I was reunited with old friends, but I had changed. I had left as a short-haired football player who wore Wranglers. I returned with long hair, wearing my NEAT Ranger beret, a Levi jacket, and 501's, carrying a double-edged boot knife tucked in my pants at the small of my back, and Nike hightops. I had been in a few fights that showed I could fight. Now, I carried an air of being downright dangerous. I was cool.

Time heals wounds, and in time, I met a new girl. This one, knowing I was interested in witchcraft, introduced me to a witch. Her name was Glasheeon. Some of her first words to me were, "You can go white magic or black magic. White magic is sorta hypocritical. If you want real power, go black magic."

"Let's go black magic." I replied.

She told me that the first step involved praying to Satan. She then gave me a special incantation to use to call forth the powers of evil. Now I was mad at God, but it still took me a day to get up the nerve to pray to the devil. That night was a turning point in my life.

By Glasheeon's instructions, I stripped naked and laid down. "Satan, I call you forth to serve you," I prayed aloud as I recited Glasheeon's incantation. I felt the room grow cold and experienced the unmistakable presence of utter evil. My pulse rate went up. The veins on my arms bulged. I experienced an erection and began to feel a lifting sensation. Then something touched me.

My eyes flew open but I saw only spots, as they had been closed so tightly. Again I felt something touch me, and I shut my eyes, feeling both terrified and thrilled. It felt like ice-cold claws began to rake my body caressingly, and I literally shook in erotic pleasure as they explored every inch of my body. I heard an audible voice speak three words in a whisper, "I love you."

I continued to pray, telling Satan I accepted and would serve him. One by one, the invisible clawed hands touching me disappeared, and my pulse rate fell. I was alone.

I sat up exhausted, hooked, unbelieving. I hadn't been on drugs. I hadn't smoked a joint. It had been incredible, and I knew it was real. I had found what I was looking for — or so I thought. The year was 1984.

I had to know more. I questioned Glasheeon crazily, learning what was myth and what was real. I went to the school library and researched biographies of prominent witches and satanists. I searched bookstores for occult-related books, often stealing those I found. I studied, I learned. And then I got my friend involved.

The more I studied, the more I became aware of the common tie binding it all together. Satan was behind D & D and behind Ninjutsu. Satan was everywhere.

Prominent men and women of society were tainted with hints of having been involved in satanism. Hitler had made a pact with Satan. It was reported that at least one famous movie star had had an affair with Anton LaVey — the author of *The Satanic Bible.* Led Zeppelin's Jimmy Page had bought Aliester Crowley's castle and owned an occult bookstore. I decided that what LaVey wrote had to be true — that Satan was the force behind rebellion which led to freedom and was a way to success in a society where only the strong survive and only the ruthless attain the American dream.

I made a pact with Satan. In my own blood I wrote, "I renounce God, I renounce Christ. I will serve only Satan. To my friends — love, to my enemies — death . . . hail Satan." I placed my name at the bottom.

I combined all I had learned into a single philosophy. The structure of D & D and CAP, the discipline and training of Zen and Ninjutsu, and the ideals, concepts, and ritualistic practices of satanism all combined to become what we called the Elimination. I hated the Christian community which I perceived to be hypocritical, and was determined to eliminate Christians from society.

Our group began performing rituals, but something seemed to be wrong. There was a barrier between us and the power we needed to invoke. We brought forth demons, but we wanted more. It was time to prove our allegiance to Satan.

We began to break the Ten Commandments one by one. Only one remained, "Thou shall not murder." We talked about ways to accomplish the goal of murder, such as waiting at a stop sign in the middle of nowhere and blowing away the first person who was fool enough to obey the law. We also talked about torture for a friend's ex-girlfriend. We would tie her down, slice her breasts, cut her throat, but only after we would rape her for a few days.

It was after a lust ritual with my second priest that Satan took over our actions. In a game-like surreal euphoria, we drove to a convenience store where a man worked who had insulted my friend's girlfriend and refused to sell him beer. In my hand I held a cold steel killing tool — a .357 magnum loaded with hollow points.

After much conversation with the man who thought we were friends, my friend distracted him and I raised the gun from beneath the counter, pointed it at his head, and squeezed the trigger. It missed. I fired again. The second shot had only injured him. My friend cut him off from getting away. I caught him.

His terror-stricken eyes searched mine for mercy behind the smoking barrel that I pointed directly at him. I squeezed the trigger and he collapsed, knocked back from the impact — dead. Blood covered the rear wall and ran onto the floor. And two teenagers walked out, taking no money, no merchandise. Only the life of an innocent man for Satan.

In the car, we laughed as the evil delight of our action gripped us. We were not human. We were completely possessed by our demonic servants. We were stripped of all love, mercy, and kindness, and were consumed with hate, anger, and eroticism. We were satanists, and we were proud of it. From our point of view, what we were doing was exciting fun. It was also very serious to us.

The rituals continued, and now the barrier was gone. I began doing solitary rituals, invoking demons and asking them to enter my body as a sanctuary. During a ritual, in sacrificing my own blood to Satan, I received my satanic name: Ezurate. Scars began to appear on my body, on my arms and chest where I continually gave blood to my master. I had begun to drink blood. I actually craved it. I took blood from my friends and myself, storing it in vials I had taken from a clinic. To keep my parents from questioning the scars, I used needles most of the time.

After a ritual in Colorado during summer vacation, we brought drugs into our coven. We got high sitting amidst cooling black candles and discarded black robes. After the fourth joint, a sense of creeping paranoia flung us from the abandoned office building we were using. A week later, I was caught shoplifting black material from a fabric store and was sent home.

I began smoking, taking speed, sniffing rush, and toking joints at school. After punching holes in the bathroom wall of a teen club called Skully's, I got a job there as a bouncer. Friday and Saturday nights were spent drinking, getting high, and partying with the 'Rockies' — the people who attended the Rocky Horror Picture Show — who frequented Skully's after the movie.

With live teenage bands rocking out the sound of "Breaking the Chains," I would sit there, wearing my black tanktop, camouflage fatigues, high tops, bandanas, and eye liner, drinking beer from plastic cups, and smoking cigarettes while my new girl-friend, Angel, would eye me from across the table wearing a black and red Spandex unitard, black knee-high boots, my white vest and black hat, and a choke collar and dog leash around her neck.

We danced, borrowed back seats from our friends before I got my pickup, and slept together. We would get high, talk about life, and remain the center of attention at Skully's.

Satanism had become our life-style. It was no longer something bragged about, or showed off. It was serious to us and it became the center of our lives. I continued to study and perform nightly rituals, taking more and more speed to keep going. The Elimination had disbanded, leaving me to pursue my own, more mature practices, including a worship of the dead, again in combination with Ninjutsu, as I searched for true enlightenment.

And here I was. But I wasn't happy. The blood, drugs, sex, hate, all of it had become boring. But I knew no other way. I had searched everywhere and I had come up empty. My life stunk. I was angry with my parents. I continually thought about suicide. I just wanted out.

I sat there in my pickup, wishing I had either the guts to blow my brains out, or some way to find a new world and leave everything behind. I had been awake for three days. I was out of speed. Tonight I would get some sleep, I planned.

I drove home, did some homework, performed a ritual, and slept. My next clear memory is a jail cell two days later. Without realizing it, I had taken my father's .44 revolver and shot both my parents in the head as they slept! It took a year, but the memories of that night eventually began to haunt me. I had stood in front of my mother's convulsing body, watching blood pour from a hole in her face, and laughing in a hideous giggle. I had felt relieved, as if the world's oppressions had been lifted from my shoulders. But for now, all I knew was that my life was destroyed.

I had given Satan everything, and now I sat in a jail cell without a family. I no longer wanted to be a satanist, and as I renounced Satan in my mind, an old familiar voice spoke with me. Suicide. I would kill myself. Only my genuine love for Angel prevented me from doing so.

Two days later a man came to the cell next to mine. He gave me a Bible and I opened it and began reading without knowing why. I had mutilated Bibles, burned them, urinated on them, poured blood on them, but now, for the first time I read one — without any ulterior motives, I read just because something seemed to say to me, "Search."

As I opened the paperback book and read from Psalms, an overwhelming sense of guilt fell upon me. I had been wrong. Satan had lied to me. It was God, not Satan, who truly loved me.

I had cursed and railed against God. I had knelt at an altar of Satan covered in blood, full of hate toward the Creator. And still, my God loved me.

I felt a new presence wanting to descend on me, crying for me to let it in. I fell to my knees and prayed really for the first time. "Lord, here I am again. If you will take me back, I will serve you."

God touched me, honoring that prayer, and I began to cry. I cried for two hours, not caring who saw me. And when I slept, it was the first peaceful night's sleep I'd had in a year and a half. I awoke knowing everything would be okay.

I had no idea what would happen. I didn't care. It didn't matter, because in that one moment all things I had searched for were found in my Jesus. I had been forgiven and given an incomprehensible peace. At that moment, I knew true love and realized all I had sought all along was only this, and finally, I was free.

Three months later, while in the county jail, I had a dream. In this dream, I awoke from a night's sleep in my room at home. I had killed no one. I was not in jail. Simultaneously, however, I had the horrible realization that I was still a satanist.

In utter humiliation and remorse, I fell to my knees and cried out to God for salvation. At the same time, my mother raced into my bedroom. As she kissed me and we embraced, I asked her to forgive me for everything I had done as a satanist. She forgave me and we cried as we continued to hug each other.

When I woke up from the dream, the harsh reality of all I had done overwhelmed me. This reality replaced my wishful dream and I began to sob. I was simply devastated. I wanted to die so I could escape the anguish of my personal reality. The pain of my remorse was far more intense than any physical anguish could ever be.

Eight months later I heard a judge read from a jury's decision, "For the crime of murder in the first degree . . . you will be sentenced to die by lethal injection."

The words hung in the air. One of the guards who had escorted me to the courtroom turned toward a window as a tear ran down his cheek. My family winced and choked back their own emotions. My friends cried, and I sat there oblivious to it all. My only thought was a simple prayer,"Very well then, Father, I'm coming home."

I walked back to my cell slowly, in a mild form of shock, and in October of 1986 I arrived at the

Oklahoma State Penitentiary and Death Row. Now, over three years later, I look back at the nightmare of my memories, and see them being recreated in the lives of others.

My first year on Death Row was spent realizing God had not ended my life with the jury's decision. I realized God still had a purpose and plan for Sean Sellers. As I began to reach out through letters to those involved in occultism I began to understand parts of that plan. This book is only the beginning.

PART II

SATANISM

Regard not them that have familiar spirits,
neither seek after wizards, to be defiled by them:
I am the Lord your God.

(Leviticus 19:31)

2

Satan's Web

Many people refuse to believe that satanists really exist. They don't believe there are those living among us who actually worship the devil. They mistakenly dismiss satanism as an excuse for people doing certain things (such as drugs). The sad fact remains that satanists do exist and they believe in what they're doing whether anyone else believes they do or not.

It is not my intention to record all of the satanic-related murders and child molestations that have occurred in recent years. There have been many around the world, and the number grows each year. Police may endeavor to "downplay" evidence of satanism in crimes due to public reaction. However, because of such an abundance of occult-related crimes, with the numbers growing each year, the police are beginning to acknowledge the existence of satanism and are learning to watch for it. Many officers attend workshops and seminars to learn the symptoms, rituals and effects of satanism.

Origins of Satanism

Satanism began after the flood of Noah in the city of Babel, which was built by Nimrod. Nimrod's kingdom — Babylon — still exists today in many different forms. The god, Marduk, is credited in mythology as being the entity who built Babel.

Nimrod set up a system of sun-god worship which has spread over the world and infested many organizations to the present day. The god Marduk is worshiped today by a group of individuals who also worship the dead. Their guidebook is the *Necronomicon* or "book of the dead." It was published for mass distribution in the early eighties. There is evidence to support the contention that the *Necronomicon* is a hoax — an imaginative book put together by H. P. Lovecraft enthusiasts. However, the book's ideals are completely evil and people, especially teenagers, have taken the book seriously enough that its rituals and practices are being performed in many places. Thus, hoax or not, Marduk is being worshiped, and Satan uses this false worship to accomplish his goals.

The sun gods or Baalistic gods were worshiped by the pagans throughout the Old Testament. For centuries these Baalistic gods were the dominant satanic influence over the world. When the followers of these gods began to infiltrate the governments of the world, a new set of followers came out of the darkness.

The Druids

During the Middle Ages in Scotland, Ireland and throughout England, the Druids or "men of oak" were the most feared group in the world. They worshiped Kernos, "the horned hunter of the night."

The most famous Druid of all is Merlin, the magician of King Arthur in Camelot.

The Druids' most important holiday was Samhain, celebrated on October 31. The Druids, dressed in cloaks, paraded boldly about the kingdoms. They chose a castle or serfdom and demanded a gift, a female virgin to be given for sacrifice. If they were given what they demanded, they left a jack-o-lantern in front of the door illuminated with a candle of human fat. If they were not appeased, they painted a hexagram on the door in blood, and during the night someone in the house would die. Today, we mimic this Druidic holiday in our Halloween traditions. The Druids still exist today in secrecy. Their only monument is the remains of Stonehenge.

As the world came out of the Dark Ages, most satanism was forced into secrecy. The only notable "above ground" worship was found in voodoo and shamanism in Africa and other unexplored "dark" countries.

Aliester Crowley

In the 1920's, Aliester Crowley situated himself on a small island with a castle. He had supposedly developed a scientific technique to govern drug use. By mathematically increasing the amount of heroin he took, it is reported that he was able to increase his daily intake of heroin to such an extent that it would have killed a full-grown bull elephant. He had the numbers "666" (the number of the anti-christ) tattooed on his forehead and urged his followers to do the same. He wrote many books which still are in print today.

Anton LaVey

After Aliester Crowley died, Anton Szandor LaVey rose to fame in the 1960's. He formed the First Church of Satan in San Francisco, an "above ground" church, and wrote *The Satanic Bible, The Satanic Rituals,* and *The Complete Witch.* These books still sell abundantly today. LaVey gave many public presentations during the sixties. His church performed satanic weddings, satanic funerals, and satanic baptisms openly.

One of LaVey's first disciples, Dr. Michael Aquino, went on to develop his own style of satanism. Whereas LaVey's style pushed theatrics and ritual, Aquino went on to develop a scientific form of worship. He is the founder of the Temple of Set (which is named for an ancient Egyptian god of the independent psyche). Aquino is also an officer in the U.S. Army Reserve. He has top-secret clearance, and is skilled in brainwashing techniques and intellectual warfare. His followers make up the leading organized national satanic group in America.

The Illuminati

Chief among the Baalistic groups that seemingly disappeared before the Dark Ages is the Illuminati. It was created in the early 1500's by a group of Europeans who maintained that their minds had been illuminated as the sun. They set up this group to infiltrate governments and control the world from within.

Although the Illuminati was created long after the Baalistic gods had seemingly disappeared, it was based on those same foundations which had remained hidden.

Freemasonry

In league with the Illuminati, it would seem, are the lodges of Freemasonry. Nimrod, who built Babel, was the founder of Freemasonry according to *The Encyclopedia of Freemasonry*, and the sun-god-type signs and worship are kept from the members of the lodges until they reach the top. The writings of Albert Pike, Sovereign Pontiff of Universal Freemasonry, declare that Satan or Lucifer — the morning star — is the god of masonry.

These groups all tie together through various sources and are, therefore, interwoven into the governments of every country of the world.

The more open forms of satanism have also gone unnoticed and unchecked by most of society. The New Age Movement, the role-playing game — Dungeons and Dragons — and the intense interest in astrology and other oracle-consulting methods are all directly related to satanism.

The New Age Movement

The New Age Movement is primarily engaged in work that has as its goal the issuing in of a one-world government. The movement is responsible for the Declaration of Interdependence and the upcoming constitutional convention. The basic teachings of the New Age are that a person can rise to a higher plane of existence through meditation, astral projection and contact with other planetary entities. Reincarnation is believed in and a person is taught to use the aspects learned in former lives to progress in this one. Many of the ideals of the Bible are also taught.

Occult Tools in Use Today

Astrology, Ouija Boards, tarot cards, runes and other forms of fortune telling are very prominent in our society. Astrological horoscopes are in nearly every newspaper in the country. Nearly every child over eight years old knows his zodiacal sign. Mrs. Reagan consulted an astrologer in an effort to keep her husband safe.

Ouija Boards are mass produced by Parker Brothers as a game and they can be found in many elementary schools across the country. Tarot cards are becoming more popular and are sold in bookstores everywhere. And the once-secret language of the Celtic runes is now common in most occult bookstores everywhere.

Even with all this, people still refuse to see or believe in satanism. Throughout the Old and New Testaments, God continually declares all forms of idolatry, spiritism, fortune telling, and magic, as evil. Satanism has become so deeply ingrained in our society that it often goes unnoticed by the untrained eye.

Fear

Today there are many people, inlcuding many Christians, who are extremely afraid of satanism. This type of paranoia only causes satanism to grow stronger. People should educate themselves concerning the practices and signs of satanism so it can be opposed, not feared.

Satanists *cannot* place hexes on Christians. They can chant, kill animals, dance, and terrorize all they wish, but curses placed on true believers are powerless and they often backfire. The Church should not give curses any recognition whatsoever.

Symptoms of Satanic Involvement

There are signs to look for that are often exhibited by people involved in the occult. Learn to watch for these signs:

—An unusual interest in the Bible without a change in behavior (many people read the Bible to learn about Satan or to blaspheme the Scriptures by mocking them or writing them backwards).
—Eating raw meat.
—Interest in occult-related movies and books.
—Talking in rhyme.
—Poems speaking of blood, murder, Satan, evil, dying or God as a mockery.
—Boys growing long fingernails.
—Accumulated scars.
—Unusually violent rebellion.
—Occult drawings on notebooks or tattoos on the body.

—Unusual type of dress, especially black clothing and occult symbols.

—Altars set up in back yards, tree houses, club houses, or bedrooms, with candles, knives, chalices, and/or occult symbols.

—Boys wearing mascara, or other makeup to look evil and/or black nail polish.

Note: The presence of one or two of these signs does not necessarily mean an individual is involved in the occult. Some may indicate involvement with heavy metal or punk music. All eventually lead to a fascination with the devil, and often, an infatuation with dying or death. You should be able to tell the difference. Don't go on a "witch hunt," however.

When these signs seem to indicate a person is involved in the occult, first, start praying for them, then single them out. Let them know they are loved. Tell them Jesus loves them. Don't be condemning or negative; be loving.

If you think it is necessary to report the person to a counselor or teacher, be sure to exercise caution. Do not make it publicly known that you are reporting a satanist unless you are held firmly in the protective grip of the Lord Jesus. Seeking revenge is as much a way of life to a satanist as forgiving is to a Christian.

Signals of Satanism in a Community

There are signs to look for in the community as well:

—Increase in the number of missing children.

—Animal mutilations.

—Occult graffiti.

—Occult-related books disappearing from bookstores and libraries.

—Bonfires and meetings in deserted places (open fields, old barns, etc.) at night, especially during the full moon.

—Mysterious murders that police refuse to talk about.

—Demand for occult jewelry in jewelry stores.

Note: The presence of these signs does not necessarily mean an active group or satanic coven is operating in the area, but they are worthy of close attention and follow-up.

If these signs seem to indicate a coven is in operation, be alert to where the group might meet, and report it to the police. If teenagers are involved, their parents should be notified, and they may need professional help from people who have experience in this field.

3

Satanic Signs and Symbols

But I say, that the things which the Gentiles sacrifice, they sacrifice to devils, and not to God; and I would not that ye should have fellowship with devils.

(1 Corinthians 10:20)

 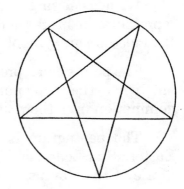

Pentagram

This is probably the most popular of all occult symbols. The five points have been related to many things. All have a similarity in that they somehow either defy God or ignore Him.

In Ninjutsu, an ancient art of assassination which has reemerged with great popularity in recent years, the five points symbolize the five elemental materials used to learn hiding or disappearing techniques: wood, metal, water, earth and air. It is also taught as a perfect symbol of nature and meditation.

In the occult, with the single point downward, the pentagram represents a fall of the "Holy Trinity," and the dual nature of Satan, power and pleasure, thrusting upward in defiance. It also represents Kernos, the horned hunter of the night, or the god Mendes.

With the single point upward, the star represents the bright and morning star of Lucifer. It is also a sun symbol.

The points can represent earth, water, fire and air, with the top point representing man's domination over them all.

The pentagram is also the symbol of the Eastern Star Lodge, and is on the covers of the first Motley Crue albums.

Sigil of Baphomet

This sign, also a pentagram, is used exclusively with the worship of Satan. It represents the being of Satan — the goat, the rival of the sacrificial Lamb of God, or the goat of Mendes.

Satan is represented as the force of nature which leads to rebellion and freedom.

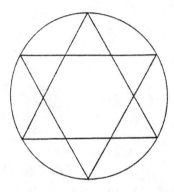

Hexagram

This is said by some to be the most powerful and evil sign in satanism, and of all the occult world. It should not be confused with the Holy Star of David, which is not occultic. It can represent the evil trinity (Satan, the Beast and False Prophet) merging with the fallen nature of man (pride, power, and pleasure).

The six points can also represent the number of the Beast of Revelation (666). The hexagram is used mainly in witchcraft to summon (call forth) demons from the underworld. The word "hex," which means to place a curse on someone, originated from this sign. It is said this was the sign the ancient Druids painted on the doors of unfortunate victims who were sacrificed during Samhain.

Crescent-Star

The crescent-star is also found in witchcraft. This symbol represents Diana (the Queen of Heaven) as the moon, and Lucifer or Nimrod or some other deity as the star. This sign is often used as a protective talisman against unwanted spirits. It is seldom used during ceremonies or rituals.

Ankh

This is the ancient Egyptian symbol of life. It represents reincarnation, and was originally used in worship of the sun god "RA." It is a sign of fertility and sex. Many witches who worship in sexually based covens will wear this symbol. It is said to be the standard Constantine placed on his soldiers in A.D. 312 when he announced himself a "Christian."

Unicorn Horn or Italian Horn

This symbol is always worn as jewelry. It represents a financial plea to the forces of nature or chance. It was created by the Druids and worn as a talisman. It is sometimes called a "fairy wand" or "leprechaun's staff."

Peace Sign

Sometimes this sign is called a trident. It represents the cross of Christ inverted and broken, which symbolizes the rejection of the Lord's sacrifice. (It is said Peter was crucified on a cross of this form because he felt unworthy to die as his Lord had died.) It can also represent an ancient rune symbol inverted. As the trident, it represents the pitchfork of Satan piercing souls, purging the world of war, by destroying the enemy from within.

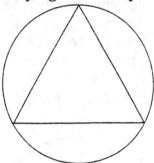

Thaumaturgic Triangle

This sign is used in witchcraft to summon demons as the hexagram and magic circle are. The demon is contained in the triangle, while the witch or warlock sits or stands outside the perimeter of the circle. It is usually seen in "white" magic, while "black" magicians usually use a pentagram.

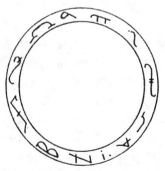

Magic Circle

This symbol, used in witchcraft, usually was drawn as a means of focusing cosmic force into one point. The practitioner would stand or sit therein while the forces he or she invoked would be contained in a triangle or hexagram.

The pentagram, thaumaturgic triangle, magic circle and hexagram are all interchangeable. Each can be used in place of the other during rituals; it is up to the individual's style and preference to determine how they are to be used. Interestingly, the pentagram, magic circle, and thaumaturgic triangle can all be found in the Dungeon and Dragon's *Dungeon Master's Guide.*

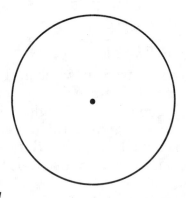

Sun Symbol

This sign is found in Freemasonry and has Baalistic origins. It is a phallic symbol (a representation of the top of the penis). Many believe the point to represent God in the center of the universe — the circle, but *The Encyclopedia of Freemasonry* by Albert Mackey, reveals: ". . . the phallus, and the point within the circle come from the same source . . . the point within a circle was first adopted by the old sun worshipers and incorporated into the symbolism of freemasonry."

Obelisk

The obelisk is another phallic symbol. This sign appears always in statue form. It represents resurrection. It is also found in Freemasonry and was originally designed as a temple for one of the ancient Baalistic gods. The Washington Monument is an obelisk.

Pyramid and Evil Eye

This sign symbolizes the eye of Lucifer watching over the finances of the world. It is one of the most powerful of spiritism or divination symbols. It is also referred to as the all-seeing eye of the Illuminati. This symbol is on the back of the American dollar bill, but was not placed there by occultists. It has a pure meaning but has been raped of this purity by generations of occultism.

There are countless other signs, but the ones we've diagramed are the most prominent in society today. These signs are seen in many places and should be a witness themselves as to how much control Satan has over the world.

James wrote, "Whosoever therefore will be a friend of the world is the enemy of God" (James 4:4). The things of the world are evil. We are forced to use the things of the world (money and government), but we are not forced to love the world. Our home is in heaven, and that is where our heart should be also.

PART III

Occultism Everywhere

So Saul died for his transgression which he committed against the Lord, even against the word of the Lord, which he kept not, and also for asking counsel of one that had a familiar spirit, to inquire of it; And inquired not of the Lord."

(1 Chronicles 10:13-14)

4

Occult Games and Talismans

Tarot Cards

Tarot Cards (pronounced ter-row) have long been the foremost tool of divination and fortune telling among occultists. The Tarot have many forms, from the Rider-Waite deck of seventy-eight, to the Witches Tarot, to basic Tarot decks of twenty-two. Recently, because of the commercial sales of these cards, the Tarot have gained much popularity.

The Tarot are a set of cards with various symbols on them. Among the symbols common to almost all Tarot decks are the death card, usually symbolizing change, and the devil card, usually symbolizing bondage. The cards are laid down in various combinations and turned over to be interpreted.

Background

The Tarot were first mentioned by the French archeologist, Court de Gebelin, at the close of the eighteenth century, and he attributed them to an Egyptian origin.

Today there is also an increasing interest in Cartouche cards which are patterned after the symbols of Egyptian religious beliefs. Immediately after de Gebelin began his discussions, a man named Alliette also took up the subject. Alliette wrote a great deal about the Tarot and endeavored to trace their connection with Egypt through the Jewish Kabbalah (a book of Oriental Jewish mysticism and numerology).

In 1855, Eliphas Levi began contributing to the occult subject. He wrote that the Tarot are a key to the esoteric tradition of the Jews and instituted an analogy between Tarot symbols and the Hebrew alphabet, the Tetragrammaton (the four-letter name of God transliterated in English as Jehovah or Yahweh), and aspects of the Jewish law.

Prophetic Divination

This may mean that the Tarot might have been a pure form of divination used by the prophets of God at one time. However, that can only be guessed at, and if it once was true, both the Tarot and the Kabbalah have gone through so many changes that neither of them today can be used to communicate with God. Any efforts to do so would be in vain because all the Tarot are completely occult in their present form.

The Tarot does indeed have Kabbalistic connections. Today it is maintained that the Kabbalah holds the true key to the Tarot, just as the Tarot holds the key to the Kabbalah. The true nature of Tarot symbolism is a secret in the hands of a very few persons. However, occultists and spiritists combine the cards as they like and attribute them as they like and their methods of using them work for divination and fortune telling.

Autohypnotic Condition

The theory of the Tarot rests upon nature. This theory acknowledges that every happening in the universe is caused by pre-established laws. The practice of Tarot is based upon the assumption that man has a prophetic gift which manifests itself through clairvoyance.

The Tarot produce an *autohypnotic condition* (identical with crystal-induced meditations) that is somewhat like a light trance. This state of mind is needed for all kinds of divination, and is something common to all the occult tools. The Tarot's "virtue" is to induce that psychic or mental state favorable to divination. That means the thing which makes the Tarot work is its ability to separate a person from his conscious mind.

One very popular Tarot card reader said she does not remember each reading because something else takes over her mind when she reads the cards. She lets the "force" do all the work; she is just a willing vessel.

It is said that the Tarot is both a generator and a battery. It gives birth to the practitioner's thoughts and also nurses them. The Tarot produce an independent and self-sufficient world, and the mind is made objective and detached.

The Tarot figures on the cards themselves do not lead to an established doctrine. In other words, a Tarot reader will never discover "Jesus is Lord" by the cards. In fact, Tarot practitioners regard all established doctrine as confining and they use the Tarot to liberate themselves and others from such "bonds."

As in astrology, the Tarot propose a method for predicting future events and man's character, and the Tarot practitioner, or diviner, wants to know what will happen in this world — how the spiritual realm will interact with man.

Origins of Occultism

All occult religious beliefs stem from ancient worship of the sun, first recorded as the Baalistic religion of Babylon. The Babyolonians built the first recorded ziggurat (a type of pyramid). It was used for observing the sun and stars.

The Babylonians were an advanced culture. Their numerical system, instead of being based on ten, was based on *sixty*. The world still uses this numerical base to measure, as the Babylonians did, time and angles: 60 minutes in an hour, 360 degrees in a circle, etc. This numerical base carried great importance in the worship of the sun god which came to be known, among many, many other names, as Baal, and the secrets of this system, called numerology, are recorded to an extent in the Kabbalah. It should be remembered that God destroyed Babylon for this idolatry.

Egypt adopted its own gods from the gods of Babylon, and the Tarot's mathematical perfections, which make the cards unique, come from the importance of numerology-based practices of worship in Babylon. These secrets found their way into Jewish mysticism, perhaps during Israel's captivity in Babylon or through the Baalistic (sun worshiping) beliefs of the forebearers of the Masonic Lodge.

Simplistically, the Tarot is a tool of sun worship, although that definition is extremely crude. The Tarot are, more accurately, a tool for worshiping or interpreting the universe.

The Tarot practitioner denies the belief in Jesus as Lord (as do the Kabbalistic Jews) and choose instead to worship the creation and not the Creator. It is this subtlety which most of the occult "games" share with the Tarot, because this is the basis of idolatry, and it is very dangerous.

Idolatry

Idolatry is simple. It is worshiping something other than God. It could be in the form of a statue as with Buddhists and Hindus; it can be the stars as astrologers do; it can be man as humanists and atheists do, or it can be the concept of good as moralists do. Idolatry is simply worshiping something other than God — the Creator.

Very often, addictions become idols in people's lives as well. Such idols usurp a position reserved for God alone.

People do not need to worship Satan overtly in order to attach themselves to the dark side. Rebellion against God is enough. By simply not worshiping God a person declares himself to be God's enemy.

The Tarot is an occult tool of ancient origin, and when it is used for divination, it becomes either an idol in and of itself, or it initiates the idolatry God forbids of His people. In that way people who use it are actually condemning themselves without realizing it.

RUNES

A Secret Alphabet

In the past 100 years, runecraft has experienced a rebirth in the framework of the magical practices of the world. The word "rune" is best defined as "secret." It originates from an old Celtic word that means "mysterium." Runes are unique in that they are inlaid with a quality of language.

In ancient times, the runes were inscribed as symbols to express basic ideas. As time went on, the symbols evolved into both a written language and a system of religion and magic. The heiroglyphical nature of the runes is important to history, and although many times the runic inscriptions were made by people who delegated to them much magical significance, runes as a language are harmless and should not be mistaken with the art of runecraft.

Runes are symbols which are cut or burned and sometimes painted on small tiles of wood, stone or metal. They are usually carried in a small bag and either dumped out, or set down systematically to be read.

Universal Applications

Much study has revealed the runes to be highly complex. They are ideographs expressing a process and flow of force and energy. This means that each rune expresses a basic idea.

For example: one rune shaped like an arrow expresses the concept of violence or war. Each rune has a threefold nature: Form (ideograph and phonetic value when in relation to runes as a language), Idea (symbolic content), and Number (revealing its relationship to other runes).

Because the runes represent universal concepts, they are easily incorporated into many magical systems. Runes summarize and graphically express separate world concepts which are used as focal points for magical and mystical operations. For example, most languages and cultures have words for the concepts of "war," "love," "doorway," etc. Rune symbols represent concepts readily understood in one's own language. Therefore, the runes are easily incorporated into magical systems around the world. A magic circle painted on the floor of two distinct cultures could bear the same Rune symbols.

In legend, runic concepts came into being before animate beings inhabited the worlds. They were given to man by Odhinn-the Viking god of magic, by an initiatory process in which the person passed through the nine worlds of the tree (by being crucified to it) and entering momentarily into the realm of Hel (death). In that moment he would be given the secrets of the runes.

Magical Origins

The runic system may well have been fully developed by as early as 200 B.C. It is important to remember that, although runes are a language in their own right, they were born from a magical origin which never left them. Some German investigators of this century have guessed that the runes actually are the origin of the Tarot system. The Tarot cards and the runic alphabet bear some interesting parallels. That would mean they are also a part of numerological worship as in Babylon.

In the past runes were used mostly as inscriptions on magical talismans, swords, doorways, etc. to give spiritual protection and psychic energy to the user.

By the nineteenth century, runecraft was almost forgotten. Certain runic symbols such as the celtic cross (see following diagram) were still common because of Christian evangelists adopting them and changing their meaning in an effort to convert people. (The Celtic cross was taken from the sun wheel — a primary worship symbol. This symbol is significant in relation to the information contained in the previous chapter about the Babylonian/Baalistic (sun-worshiping) origins of the Tarot's numerological concepts, and the possible runic influence on the origins of the Tarot).

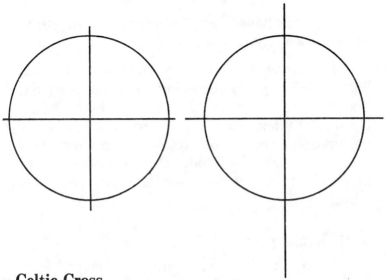

Celtic Cross

This diagram graphically illustrates how many occult symbols and concepts have seeped into the Christian Church. Many practices of Christendom have their foundations in occultism and paganism.

In 1902, a Pan-Germanic mystic named Guiddo von List remained in darkness, with his eyes bandaged for several months because of a cateract operation. During this time, he received a spontaneous runic initiation like that of the rune legend. He entered into Hel where the "secrets of the runes" were revealed to him.

As a result, he formed the Guiddo von List Society to support investigations which were directed at what he called the restoration of "*Armanentum*." He also formed the *Armanen Orden* to carry out the esoteric, or secret, functions of his new society, which were basically political in nature, and based on Anti-Semitism (against Jewish theology or culture).

List developed a magical rune system which became influential in bringing about the National Socialist movement in Germany with the racist German Orden, and he wrote several books outlining his teachings. His *Armanen Orden* was able to shape the runic theories of German magicians to the present day. Thus runecraft was reborn.

Nazi Germany

In the thirties, a new runic movement began to shine as the Nazi period began. During the Nazi regime everything "Germanic" was "placed on a pedestal" and used for manipulative purposes. Although there was much perversion in the concepts associated with runic symbols, the universality of the runes prevailed and a state-controlled system of magic developed. It is known that Hitler and many of his top officials were satanists. It is likely that the runes were used in their rites.

After the war, the *Armanen* system of runes became almost "traditional" in Germanic circles, and formed a valid and working magical system. Although it went through a reformation, the Armanen system is regarded as non-traditional, and to some extent, it is cut off from the innate powers present in the ancient runes and their system. This means that Von List (or someone after him) changed the symbolism of the runes to their own (racial?)

concepts instead of the ancient universal ones. For this reason there has recently arisen an intense study in runecraft in an effort to rediscover those lost meanings and powers.

The Asatruarmenn

On May 16, 1973, the Asatruarmenn was founded in Iceland. This represented the concrete formation of the movement that has become known as either Asatru or Odinism. There are, at present, three major Asatru groups across the world. The organizations are primarily religious in orientation and closely linked with what has become known as the New Age movement. This guild of the Asatru is dedicated to the teaching of runecraft and to a program of initiatory magical development. Basically they teach people how to be magicians in the arts of Runecraft and Odinism.

The runes are a highly complex and redeveloping form of magic. As their hidden powers have yet to be fully realized, there can be no true estimate of their danger in regards to such forces as Progressive Entrapment, however, their danger in the matter of spiritual choice should be easily recognized.

I found it very easy to incorporate rune symbols into my satanic rituals. The rune symbols for flow ⊬ and non-aggression ⅄ carry a great many different meanings in the circles of satanism. The so-called peace symbol ☮ is regarded by satanists as an upside-down, broken cross. The swastika ⊬ denotes racism. (Incidentally, it is changes like these that the Astruarmenn is trying to isolate so as to restore the rune symbols to their true meanings. By so doing they can be used in magic more effectively).

The runes have stemmed from the ancient magical practices of sun-worshiping religions. Whatever their true nature is, it is certain that they are not of God. They are surrounded with a disturbing mysterium unlike most of the normal secretive aspects of occultism. They are found in almost every country in the world — including North America — in the form of ancient heiroglyphic writings, many of which cannot be accurately deciphered.

Runes are the oldest form of occult knowledge and magic. They were perhaps the initial development of worship by those who first rebelled against God, and later never cared to seek Him out. If that is so, the practice of runecraft is rooted in direct opposition to the Creator. This could explain the universality of their concepts among all other religions, and why they have now resurfaced in an age when Jesus Christ is the only offending name in religion. Their use sets a person against God.

CRYSTALS

Theosophy

On November 17, 1875, Madame Helena Patrova Blavatsky merged various occult movements into the *Theosophical Society* and thus was reborn a seed which today has sprouted into what is called the New Age Movement. This movement is based on the belief that mankind is between ages — the Piscean Age, during which Christianity was introduced, and the Age of Aquarius. It is during the Age of Aquarius that the "evolution of religion" will take its next step forward. That step, in the eyes of New Agers, is *humanism*. This involves the belief in mankind or "self" as God.

The New-Age Movement

New Agers believe that all religions share the same basic premises, and they look forward to the time when all will unite into a universally recognized "truth" and, therefore, bring about peace upon the planet.

New Age author Marilyn Forgeson has estimated that ten million Americans are engaged in at least some aspect of Eastern mysticism. In an August 19, 1987, *Los Angeles Times* article, Shirley MacLaine states: "We seem to be going through a cleansing process in our country, with corruption and the bereavement of ethics being exposed on all levels. It's as though we are being directed to 'go within' for our own salvation and integrity."

Therein lies the basic doctrine of the New Age: to look within ourselves for the answers to all things. This concept is not new. It is an integral part of Zen Buddhism and it is present in almost all of the philosophical aspects of the martial arts.

Among New Age beliefs are the following doctrines: 1.) All is one, and all is God, and God is all. (God is, therefore, according to this belief, a coconut, a tree, the earth, the universe, and/or the self.) 2.) The belief that the Law of Karma determines life. (Karma is the culminating value of all of one's life actions, good and bad, which together determine one's next birth and life, death and rebirth. This Hinduistic idea basically means that if you are an evil person in this life, you will be born deformed or something in the next life, or if you are a good person in this life, you will be born as someone better in the next life). 3.) The belief in reincarnation. 4.) And the belief that Jesus Christ spent some time in India studying under a Buddhist or Hindu yogi.

The emergence of the self as a god or as *God* is the primary goal of each New Ager. To recognize yourself as God and attain harmony with the universe, many different exercises and meditations are taught.

Many of these meditations come from Hinduism. In India (the birthplace of Hinduism), each morning more than half a million people trek to the shores of the putrid Ganges River to bathe in the green, murky sewage, perform their meditations, and worship statues as the sun rises. New Agers teach Transcendental Meditation, visualization techniques, breathing and word mantras, and *crystal enhancement*. All of these, again, are not of God.

The Talisman of the Eighties

Crystals have become the new talisman of the eighties. Instructional books, videos, and cassette sales have risen dramatically during the past five years and the public now buys $100 million worth of crystals a year. In 1985, quartz crystal grossed $350,000. In 1987, it reached more than $1 million and is now reaching towards the $250 million mark worldwide.

A crystal is a simple, although beautiful, polished and sometimes specially cut, piece of quartz that is sold as jewelry. Larger pieces we used for holding during meditation. The crystals themselves are harmless; it is what is done with them that is dangerous.

Crystal Meditation

The categories of crystal meditation are growing. They range from crystal *chakra* balance, a meditation involving the amplification of colored light, to crystal enhancement (subliminal programing). There is also the meditation of "crystal energy" with New Age music. The teaching is that crystals are amplifiers and enhancers of mental or spiritual energy.

When crystals are used in meditation they produce an *autohypnotic condition* like a light trance. The autohypnotic condition is common in all eastern meditations. It is a way of clearing the mind of all thought and predetermined doctrines and seeking out one's own "truth." Again, the crystals themselves do nothing. In fact, any shiny object from a candle flame to a drop of water will produce this same condition. Deliberately opening oneself to various "powers" is a very dangerous choice indeed.

The meditative state itself is not the problem or concern. Many Christians will enter into meditation during their prayers. The dangers are found in the thoughts New Agers are entertaining. When in this meditative state, nothing has a definition to them. There is no good or evil; only energy. And, whatever brings about a feeling of peace is regarded as desirable.

Perceptions change what man regards as truth. (For example, we once believed the world was flat.) But to believe that truth itself, as a concept, is subject to individual perception and to believe that there are no absolutes — no unchanging good or evil — is not only dangerous, but totally ludicrous.

The New Age Movement itself is in complete opposition to Christianity. New Agers, in their belief in nothing absolute, have a blatant disregard for the Scriptures. New Age author, David Spangler, in *Emergence: Rebirth of the Sacred,* has written, "We can take all the laws, and all the marshmallows, and have a jolly good bonfire and marshmallow roast, because that is all they are worth.

"Once you are the law, once you are the truth, you do not need it externally represented to you. Rather, you will be the external representative for the world."

All of this is a form of idolatry. It is the worship of the self as God, or more broadly, it is a worship of humanity as God (humanism). This is the rebirth of the same rebellion that created Babylon, and this is completely against God.

5

Dungeons and Dragons

History of the Game

Many controversies have arisen over fantasy role-playing games. The foremost game of this type is "Dungeons and Dragons" (also known as D & D). Many questions have been raised concerning this game. Should Christians play the game? Is it morally corruptible? Is it dangerous in any way?

For the Christian, all these questions can be answered easily by locating the source from which the game stems. As in most things, if the ideals represented by the game are good, then the source of the game is God and it is, therefore, approved by God. If the ideals represented by the game are evil, then the source of the game is Satan, and, therefore, it is condemned by God. Let's take a look at what the game entails.

D & D was created by a historical war enthusiast named Gary Gygax. In 1973, he invested $1,000 into an idea and created TSR Hobbies. In 1974, Brian Blume added $2,000 to Gygax's idea and the two began to print rule books. In 1975, TSR was incorporated.

It took a year for the first 1,000 units of the game to be sold and over the next four years sales gradually grew, as popularity did.

In 1979, an explosion of publicity was centered on TSR and D & D with the sudden disappearance of a sixteen-year-old mathematical genius from Michigan State University, named James Dallas Egbert. Egbert had been playing an impromptu/drama variation of D & D in the underground college steam ventilation tunnels. He was found a short time later.

In 1979, TSR had made $2.3 million in sales. In 1980, after the publicity caused by Egbert's disappearance, TSR's sales jumped to $8.7 million. In 1981, sales generated $14 million.

Approximately a year after Egbert was found, he committed suicide. He had reportedly lost his sense of reality because of his obsession with D & D. Nothing was said of his death by the creators of the game. By 1985, TSR was making $100 million in sales.

Blume and Gygax continued to expand, revise, and update their project. They began to publish *Dragon Magazine* to supplement their game ideas. They created new and more complicated worlds or "dungeon modules," manuals on monsters, gods, legends, characters, etc. They created small lead figures for players to use for visualization during the game, and seemingly a continuing, unending array of other ideas and accessories.

The Game Itself

The game, even at the basic level, is extremely complicated. It consists of at least three players.

(Most groups have about five to nine participants.) Players begin by rolling up "characters."

D & D uses a set of multi-sided dice. There is a four-sided, six-sided, twelve-sided, twenty-sided and thirty-sided die. Using a pre-printed TSR "character sheet," players roll the six-sided die three times, adding the sum to determine scores for strength, intelligence, wisdom, dexterity, constitution, and charisma. Using suggested tables in the rule book, players choose their character's profession from the list of palladin, fighter, magic user, illusionist, Druid, cleric, thief, or assassin. Then, also using different charts, each player chooses his character's race, from a list of: human, elf, dwarf, half-elf, or half-orc.

According to his profession, each player rolls a certain die to determine his character's *hit points*. Hit points determine how much damage a character can sustain before dying. Another chart is checked for *saving throws* (to be explained later).

A player then chooses the type of person his or her character will be. This is known as *alignment*. These are chosen from three classes: lawful, neutral, chaotic and then combined with one of two subclasses: good or evil. Lawful good characters are usually honor-bound palladins (knights) who are required to follow the code of chivalry. Chaotic, evil characters are usually assassins.

After rolling the six-sided die three times and multiplying by ten, to determine the number of gold coins the character begins with, a series of charts and lists are observed from which the player buys weapons, foods, tools, supplies, and armor for each character. Hair color, eye color, sex, weight, tastes, prejudices and fears are also recorded on the character sheet. Clerics choose the deity or deities he or she will serve, and magic users, illusionists and Druids choose their spells. Strength is weighed against total weight carried by each character to determine that character's walking and running speed. And finally, the character will be given a name.

The Object of the Game

The prime object of the game is survival and the gathering of power and treasure. Each group will have secondary objects from exploring a series of caves, to finding a magical talisman in an enchanted forest, to raiding a city or town. Players assume the roles of their characters and are led through forests, mountains, caves, swamps, and cities by the *Dungeon Master* (DM). The DM is god, guide, opponent, friend, and referee to the players. The DM assumes the roles of the deities, monsters, and non-player characters encountered by the players during the adventure. Set before the DM, where the players cannot see, are various charts, dice, graphs, maps and papers needed to guide the game.

The game runs in a series of turns. Each turn is approximately ten minutes of fantasy world time and consists of the DM explaining to the group their surroundings and any action around their character's abilities to see, hear, smell or feel. Each player consults the others and allows a group leader to tell the DM what decisions and actions the characters of the group make or take.

When enemies are encountered, the play changes from turns to rounds. There are ten rounds for every turn. Each round consists of a single decision or action by each player. For instance, during a game, the DM may say, "As the door opens, suddenly a hobgoglin stands up in the middle of the room from the chair beside a table."

A group might respond, "Gandalf draws his sword, while Bomley prepares a magic missile spell. Ventura notches an arrow in her bow."

DM: "The hobgoblin picks up a battle axe and charges you."

Players: "Ventura shoots her arrow and Gandalf strikes toward the hobgoblin's head with his sword."

Ventura's dexterity score is taken by the DM. A *saving throw,* which is the added circumstance of chance in all fights, is rolled for the hobgoblin. 1-3 the arrow misses, 4-6 the arrow hits. A roll of five is made.

From another chart the arrow's damage (1-4) is measured against the hobgoblin's *armor class.* An armor class is the degree of strength the armor contains. The hobgoblin's armor class subtracts two from each hit. A roll of three is made with the four-sided die, and the arrow does one point of damage.

Gandalf's strength score is taken, which, at eighteen, gives Gandalf a bonus of two on every strike. Another saving throw is cast, missed, and the sword's damage (4-16) is rolled, measured against the hobgoblin's armor class, added bonus points to a score of ten and twelve points of damage is done. The hobgoblin had only fourteen hit points, thirteen are taken, and so the DM announces: "Ventura's arrow distracted it long enough for Gandalf to strike it across the throat, ripping out the front of its neck and jawbone. The hobgoblin falls to the ground."

And so each decision or movement continues in such extreme detail throughout the game. A game can last for years. It ends only when the Dungeon module is finished — meaning when all treasure has been found and all lands have been mapped or the purpose of the quest has been attained — or when all characters are killed.

How Satan Moves In

There is a very thin line between the players and the characters they visualize and become in the game. Each character is everything that the player can make it. What ideals are the players in the game being encouraged to uphold? By the game's own rules — murder, theft, violence and polytheistic worship are all extensive parts of D & D, as well as magic, divination, and sorcery. Each of these things is acted out in the minds of the players. Anything that leads to self-gratification is legal in the game. Mercy, morals, and loyalty give way to greed and power.

Interestingly, these same ideals are recorded in a book called *The Satanic Bible,* written by high priest of the First Church of Satan, Anton LaVey. It reads:

> Satan represents vengeance instead of turning the other cheek.

> Satan represents indulgence instead of abstinence.

> Satan represents all of the so-called sins, as they all lead to physical, mental or emotional gratification.

On Tuesday, May 12, 1987, the National Coalition on Television Violence issued a press release which read:

> The controversy around fantasy role-playing games, most notably "Dungeons and Dragons," continues to grow in the U.S. and other countries. *Ninety deaths* have now been linked to a heavy involvement with these violence-oriented, fantasy war games. These include sixty-two murders, twenty-six suicides, and two deaths of undetermined causes.

The press release goes on to record and document each of those ninety by name and incident.

Patricia Pulling, of Bothered About Dungeons and Dragons (BADD) has found thirty-seven instances where D & D has clearly played the *decisive* role in death.

Although I must disagree with some of Patricia's conclusions and state that D & D has not had quite the decisive role the National Coalition on Television Violence maintains, there is enough honest concern to give their declarations space.

The problem with D & D is not so much the violence; granted, the violence does have an effect on the players, but the real danger of D & D is found in its obsessive affinity with occultism. Occult practices play such an important role in the structure of the game (for example, every player/character must choose a pagan deity to serve) that there can be no separation from it.

Role-Playing Games

It is important to realize, however, that role-playing games in general are not destructive. Frequently, they are a kind of adults' "Let's play make believe." It is when this make believe becomes engrossed with occult symbols and practices and evil ideals that such a game holds great potential to become a source of destruction.

6

The Ouija Board

Of all the occult "games," the Ouija Board is perhaps the most dangerous, because it is uniquely thought of and packaged as a game. This is very misleading. The word "Ouija" comes from the French "Oui" and the German "Ja" — both words mean "yes," and so it is accurate to translate "Ouija" as the "yes-yes board."

Background

For those who believe the Ouija is only a game, a look into the board's history will be helpful. It has been around much longer than most people realize. The Ouija was used in the days of Pythagoras, about 540 BC, but no single person or culture can take credit for its development.

The concepts behind its mechanics and its origins are varied and ancient, and have been independently reinvented and rediscovered in a wide variety of locations.

The Ouija has become a universal folk instrument. It existed in China before the birth of Confucius (approx. 551-479 BC), in Rome in the third century, and in North America long before Columbus's arrival. (Native Indians used it to determine when and how religious ceremonies should be performed.)

The Parker Brothers version of the Ouija Board, the version most people are familiar with, was purchased in 1966 from William Fuld, who, upon the Board's advice, had bought its patent from Elijah J. Bond in 1892. Fuld made a fortune selling it through his Baltimore Talking Board Company.

The first year Parker Brothers sold more than two million Ouija Boards, topping the sales of their best-selling board game, "Monopoly."

In a court case against the Internal Revenue Service in 1920, the Baltimore Talking Board Company maintained the Ouija was *not* a game. The court's decision, written by Judge Knapp, was that the Ouija Board "is unique, in a class by itself, plainly different and distinguishable from any of the enumerated games!"

The Ouija Board is used to contact the spiritual realm. The Baltimore Talking Board Company maintained, as their attorney wrote, "[It is] a medium of communication between this world and the next." In a 1983 national Ouija Board survey, more than 30 percent of the respondents used the board to communicate with the dead. Another 30 percent tried to contact living people. The rest attempted to reach "nonhuman intelligences" in order to try to find lost objects or develop psychic abilities.

So what exactly is a Ouija Board? There are various forms, as just explained, for it *has* come up in almost every society in the world at one time or another. Usually it is a flat board, often smooth and polished, with numbers, letters, and the words "yes" and "no" painted on or sometimes cut into it. A pointer, sometimes a metal, wooden, or glass, more often plastic triangle (or heart) is placed on the board. Usually two or more people put their fingers on the pointer and slide it across the board. Questions are answered by the pointer spelling out words, numbers, or stopping on "yes" or "no."

Unexplainable Stories

There have been many unexplainable accounts which have occurred with the Ouija Board. During World War II, the noted composer, Rudolf Friml, used the Ouija Board to talk to dead composers, among them Chopin and Victor Herbert, who, he claimed, helped him write music.

During the Vietnam War a seventeen-year-old girl was told by the Ouija Board that her boyfriend, a soldier, had been shot at by another G.I. It described details to her which she recorded in a letter and sent to him. The details were accurate. He had indeed been shot at *while the letter was in the mail.*

In one of my own experiences with the board at a small party, the Ouija Board told us to go home because someone was going to get hurt. Later that night a friend of mine was hit in the mouth with a beer bottle, breaking his jaw. The person who hit him was not supposed to have been there and did not even know us.

Stories like this are common. It is such a continual source of mystery that scientists, theologians, parapsychologists, and philosophers often engage in debate to establish a common definition for the nature of the board. Despite this, most will agree that the board *is* used to contact the unknown. The spiritual realm is that unknown, and the board is *not* contacting God. That leaves only one other choice.

Progressive Entrapment

The danger of the Ouija Board is that it provides — like all oracle-consulting tools, a focus point for the spiritual dark side to enter a person's life. A method called *Progressive Entrapment* is used by the spirit entities spoken to, in order to consume the will of the person who is contacting them. Progressive Entrapment is a slow process through which evil forces change and inhabit a human being.

Progressive Entrapment begins with a subtle desire to use the board more and more. The more the Ouija Board is used, the more results are gleaned from it. That subtle desire may slowly turn into an obsession until the Ouija-invoked entities actually control the person. As the powers of these entities become stronger, personality disorders may develop and the user's mind becomes distorted, especially concerning concepts such as right and wrong. In time, the user will depend completely upon the Ouija for every decision he or she makes and will be totally obedient to the board's instructions.

Just as there are many mystery stories involving Ouija, there are also many horror stories. One of these stories tells of an eleven-year-old girl who suddenly turned from being happy and gregarious into a terrified child who was afraid to leave her home because the Ouija told her she was to be struck dead.

In 1935, upon the advice of the Ouija Board that her seventy-seven-year-old husband had given $15,000 to a woman with whom he was having an affair, a Mrs. Nellie Hurd, in Kansas City, began to systematically beat, burn, and torture him. Unable to convince his wife that the board was lying, he killed her in desperation. Both of these are results of Progressive Entrapment.

There are also accounts of trained occultists, witches, and satanists using the board as a powerful tool for contacting specific spirits or demons, and for recruiting others into their groups or covens.

When I was a satanist the Ouija was used frequently as a way to introduce individuals into the occult. We knew the Ouija was accepted by most people as being harmless, and once we got a person playing, it was only a matter of time before they would agree to join us in a satanic ritual.

Ouija Boards that have caused intense family problems have been burned, and families present have reported hearing hideous voices screaming as the flames consumed the "game."

To those involved in the occult, the Ouija is *not* a game. To them it is a powerful tool of spiritual contact foolishly regarded as a game by the ignorant.

I knew a girl who had a Ouija Board which belonged to her grandmother. The board was her most prized possession and she could actually summon demons with it by name.

The Ouija is used by those involved in the occult because it *is* a powerful tool that is *not of God*. Those who play with the Ouija foolishly open themselves and their families to occultic oppression, spiritual rebellion, and the danger of eternal damnation.

By choosing the Ouija, people reject God. It is a form of divination and the person using it is both calling to the forces of the dark side or to the dead and the medium by which they come to dwell. That means a person using a Ouija Board actually asks demons to come into their bodies, move their hands, and tell them things. And in that way the user of the Ouija Board chooses Satan over God.

7

ASTROLOGY

What Astrology Is

Astrology is the belief that the destinies of nations and individuals are determined by the relative positions of the stars. Today there are over 175,000 part-time astrologers and 10,000 full-time astrologers in the United States. Over 2,000 newspapers carry daily horoscopes, and estimates for those who believe in astrology in America run from 32 million to half the country's population. Astrology jewelry, posters, T-shirts, vending machines, etc. gross several hundred million dollars a year.

Babylon's Idolatry

The ziggurat of Babylon was constructed to view the sun, stars and moon as Babylon's form of idolatrous worship. It was for this rebellion that Babylon, the city, was destroyed. Throughout the Bible, God condemned the worship of astrological gods and Israel's final fall was linked to it as well!

> They forsook all the commands of the Lord their God and made for themselves two idols in the shape of calves, and an asherah pole. They bowed down to all the starry hosts and they worshipped Baal . . . therefore the Lord rejected all the people of Israel.

> (2 Kings 17:16 and 20)

The Zodiac

Astrology grew to be recognized as a science that applied not only to nations, but also to individuals. In the *Tetrabiblos*, Ptolemy finalized the zodiac method of casting horoscopes by the position of the sun. Astrology was no longer only for guidance regarding planting and harvest, or ritualistic holidays for worship, it could now be applied to guide each individual's life.

The zodiac is made up of twelve signs corresponding to a number of stars visible to the naked eye. As the earth revolves around the sun, the night sky changes and different stars are seen. The sign corresponding to the most prominent stars at the time of a person's birth determine what kind of person he or she will be, and guide that person's life.

The late nineteenth century marked the rebirth of the ancient art as a decline in formal religion occurred due to secularization. With the revival of occult religions and the spread of Theosophy (the precursor of the New Age movement), astrology returned and was immediately taken up by revolutionary-minded youth.

Polytheism and Idolatry

Astrology is spiritually dangerous because it is a form of polytheism (the worship of many gods). It is also a form of idolatry, because it teaches people to consult the stars (the creation) instead of God (the Creator) when there is a need for guidance.

Astrology has consumed the lives of many people. There are some who are so dedicated to the consultation of the stars that they will not get out of bed without first checking their horoscopes. Should that horoscope tell them of possible misfortune, they will not leave their homes that day.

In my own practices zodiac signs were used as part of satanic rituals.

A very interesting aspect of astrology that few understand is that it is God who created the stars, and the zodiac, when interpreted correctly, declares the plan of God to the world! The zodiac is not for man to worship or draw guidance from, it is there instead to help man understand the plan of God.

God Rules the Zodiac

Canst thou bind the sweet influences of Pleiades?... Canst thou bring forth Mazzaroth in his season? or canst thou guide Arcturus with his sons? Knowest thou the ordinances of heaven? canst thou set the dominion thereof in the earth?
(Job 38:31-33)

Lift up your eyes on high, and behold who hath created these things, that bringeth out their host by number; he calleth them all by names by the greatness of his might, for that he is strong in power, not one faileth.
(Isa. 40:26)

What message is so important that God would write it in the very stars of man? The message of God's plan to send the one who is called the Coming One; *Hamashia Mashiac,* Jesus Christ, the Messiah!

The zodiac, beginning not with Leo as common astrology teaches, but instead with Virgo, speaks of the virgin by whom the Son of God is born. Libra tells of the balance — the price paid for sin. Scorpio, the mortal conflict, sets forth Christ as wounded for our rebellion. Sagittarius, the final triumph, portrays the dualistic nature of Jesus as the God-man. (His arrow is aimed at Scorpio — Satan.) Capricornus, life out of death, symbolizes our life through the death of Christ. Aquarius, blessing out of victory, shows forth the life-giving water poured out to God's people, through the Spirit of God. Pisces represents deliverance of all nations from the slavery of sin. Aries, glory out of humiliation, is the Lamb of God who now rules creation. From Him springs Taurus, symbolizing His glorious return in surprising power. Gemeni represents His union with the Bride. Cancer, His possessions held secure, assuring nothing will escape His grasp. And Leo, the lamb who is now lion, overcoming all His enemies. (For additional study on this aspect of astrology see the book list in the Appendix.)

Astrology has been perverted, and worshiping the stars or looking for guidance from them will lead only to confusion and destruction. The message, however, is written in the very stars. If they *are* to guide us, they will guide us to our God, for only He can truly direct our paths.

PART IV

Issues Facing Youths Today

Now the works of the flesh are manifest, which are these; Adultery, fornication, uncleanness, lasciviousness, Idolatry, witchcraft, hatred, variance, emulations, wrath, strife, seditions, heresies, Envyings, murders, drunkenness, revellings, and such like: of the which I tell you before, as I have also told you in time past, that they which do such things shall not inherit the kingdom of God.

(Galatians 5:19-21)

8
Drugs and Alcohol

Every teenager, almost without exception, faces the temptations presented by drugs and alcohol. Many aren't sure about how to handle the problem. They don't know what to do in the face of the temptation, and they may be not sure how bad drugs really are. Their peers (friends) may lead them to believe that drugs and alcohol are harmless.

America's drug and alcohol problems are responsible for more deaths than all the world's wars. We can talk about drug and alcohol use or drug and alcohol abuse, but we must remember that all abuse begins with use. The difference is found in the degree of impact and effect the individual experiences.

Causes

Drug and alcohol use may begin in young people because of peer pressure from friends. Others start because of adoration of personal heroes. Still others see drugs and alcohol as a means to relax from stress, to have fun and feel good. Rebellion causes some to use these substances simply because they were told not to. Many current studies indicate that some people have an addictive personality that may lead them into drug and alcohol use.

According to the U.S. Department of Health and Human Services: "Low self-esteem is a critically important factor. Young people suffering from low self-esteem are often unable to resist peer pressure to use drugs, they also find that drugs provide them with the 'good feelings' that they lack. Young people themselves often state that their reasons for using drugs are that they're bored and have nothing better to do. In the same vein, young people also report that they use drugs because they enjoy getting high (i.e. drug use is fun, a form of recreation, a way to expand one's consciousness or enhance pleasure.)

Use Leads to Abuse

After drug use begins it very often leads to abuse. When drug use becomes common or habitual, it becomes a crutch or a refuge for the user in times of problems and stress. Ironically, while the user thinks his pressures are being alleviated, additional problems and stresses result from drug use, and so a self-destructive cycle is set in motion. More stress, more drugs, more stress, etc.

When drug use becomes drug abuse, it very quickly becomes the leading and controlling force in the abuser's life. This is when addiction sets in and it will not let the abuser go. More drugs are needed and the abuser (addict) may do anything necessary to obtain them.

Alcohol is a drug just like all the others. It presents the greatest problem to society because it is legal and it is socially acceptable. Alcohol-related traffic accidents, which account for 50 percent of all traffic fatalities, are the number-one cause of death for teenagers and young adults. Alcohol-related traffic accidents have killed more Americans in two years than the number of fatalities in the ten years of the Vietnam War. People are still upset about the war because "it was senseless." Do we fail to see the senselessness of alcohol-related traffic fatalities? According to S.A.D.D. (Students Against Driving Drunk) every twenty-three minutes an innocent person becomes the victim of a drunk driver.

More and more teenagers are becoming full-fledged alcoholics. In New York State, a series of surveys were taken. The results declare that one in every ten high school/junior high students in the area studied is "hooked on alcohol." More boys became alcoholics than girls. Beer and wine cooler commercials glorify drinking, leading many to take their first drink. Recent studies reveal that the tendency toward alcoholism may be inherited. The inheritance is passed from father to son more often than from mother to daughter. Once the youth begins to drink, inspired by the commercials and peer pressure, alcoholism takes over speedily.

Alcohol is killing our youths, and yet we are not stopping our consumption of the poison.

Marijuana

The use of marijuana is the next most popular form of drug abuse. Many maintain that marijuana is not harmful to the body, but its smoke contains more cancer-causing substances than equivalent amounts of tobacco. It quickens the heart rate and may cause irregular heart rhythms. It also affects the endocrine system, the glands, and the hormones that control normal growth, energy, and reproduction. It reduces sperm production and mobility. It can stop the menstrual cycle, and research is now reporting chromosome damage which will affect future generations. In short, the idea that marijuana isn't harmful is a myth. The fact is, it messes you up! It also leads to other drugs.

Psychologically, when one drug is accepted, usually marijuana (and alcohol) first, it becomes easier to accept other drugs. Marijuana doesn't *seem* to harm you. It dries out your eyes and mouth and gives you an incredible appetite when coming down from it, but no other effects are felt other than the high it produces. The user will begin to subconsciously think that other drugs are also not harmful, because they don't see any damage being done to their bodies. This erroneous thinking leads them to accept the other drugs.

Stimulants

The next drug in the cycle is usually speed, or some other stimulant or amphetamine. Speed gives the user an excessive amount of energy and stamina. Because marijuana creates a sense of drowsiness and lack of strength, the user may take speed to counteract the effects of pot. Speed comes in two different forms: pills and powder. It can be swallowed, sniffed, or dissolved in water and injected into the veins.

Regardless of how it is taken, speed causes tension and stress, speeds up the heart rate, and creates a false hyperactive state. When coming down from it, it drains the body of all energy and so becomes mentally addictive. When the user comes down, he will need more to bring him back up. It's not uncommon for a user to smoke a joint and take speed at the same time. The result is a mellow, yet energetic stupor.

Cocaine

After speed, cocaine may follow. Frank LaVecchia, a former high school guidance counselor who runs a drug treatment center in Miami, Florida, says: "There are two trends in cocaine use: younger and younger, and more and more." In the past, cocaine was an expensive "high-class" drug. Today, with the easy distribution of smokeable cocaine (called "crack"), it is the most readily available drug besides alcohol, marijuana and speed.

Dealers make crack by mixing cocaine with baking soda and water, forming a paste which hardens and is broken into "rocks." A small rock, usually smoked in a pipe, creates a twenty-to-thirty-minute euphoria, but it is deadly. Arnold

Washington, a psycho-pharmacologist in Summit, New Jersey, said, "Crack is the most addictive drug known to man right now. It is almost instantaneous addiction, whereas, if you snort coke it can take two to five years before addiction sets in. There is no such thing as the 'recreational use' of crack."

Between 1981 and 1985, cocaine-related deaths in twenty-five major metropolitan centers more than doubled, and cocaine-related emergency room visits tripled. According to *U.S. News and World Report,* Americans now consume 60 percent of the world's production of illegal drugs. An estimated 20 million people are regular users of marijuana, four to eight million are cocaine abusers, and 500,000 are heroin addicts. "The time has come to give notice that individual drug use is threatening the health and safety of all our citizens," President Ronald Reagan stated on July 30, 1986. The echo of his words is stronger now — four years later.

Drugs have claimed the lives of many prominent singers, actors, and entertainers such as: John Belushi, Sid Vicious, Keith Moon, Jimi Hendrix, Judy Garland, and Janis Joplin. Why is it that people who seem to have it all, still kill themselves with drugs? The answer is simple.

Drugs and Occultism

Satan can create nothing. He can only pervert what God creates. Because God created us with a desire to seek Him and to know Him, we are always searching for something.

Satan uses drugs as an answer to fill that empty spot within us that only God can fill. He uses drugs to blind and bind people from the truth, to destroy their bodies and minds, and eventually kill them.

Drugs are inherently connected to occultism. From the earliest times, in almost every pagan culture, priests or medicine men have used drugs as an important part of elaborate ceremonies, for spiritism, and to control others. Removing the religious aspects of drug use does not remove the results. The binding force behind drugs, which robs people of their free will and ability to choose, is against God.

The Lord has said that the body is the temple of the Holy Spirit, and Satan will do all he can to destroy that potential temple.

"What? know ye not that your body is the temple of the Holy Ghost which is in you, which ye have of God, and ye are not your own?" (1 Cor. 6:19).

9
Sex

Media Exploitation

Sex has become the most popular subject in our society. Exploitation of the body, and the sexual act is reflected in television, movies, books, magazines, and advertisements. Even such perversions as homosexuality, bestiality, and sex with children (pedophilia) have made a direct impact on our society, and created problems never faced before.

Sex plays one its most dominant roles on television. Daily dramas or "soap operas" (called that because the early shows were supported by soap advertisements) are based almost wholly on sex. They also glorify certain crimes and sins such as blackmail, murder, adultery and foster attitudes that lead to jealousy, envy, greed and materialism.

These programs are supposedly reflections of our true society, and to a degree they are. They are, however, focused on the evils of society. Although society is evil, very few, if any real people lead a life like that of J. R. Ewing. Most soap opera families are rich or at least wealthy, while most in society are not.

Soap opera writers use "cliff hanger" endings for each episode to "grab" and "keep" viewers interested. Competition between the networks is fierce and this method is employed to maintain viewer loyalty. This results in a form of psychic addiction. Once a viewer becomes interested in a program, it is very hard to break away from it. The curiosity of "what's going to happen to Bobby" keeps the viewer returning. In so doing, he returns to nothing more than pure evil time and time again.

Television movies and talk shows are often sexually oriented also. Major television productions and specials have "progressed" from the MGM classic adventures to simply more dramatic soap operas.

In recent years even masturbation has been introduced into children's vocabularies. In the name of openness and sex education, children learn about sexuality in an atmosphere without moral values. For example, if a teenager does not masturbate he is said to be sexually repressed. Similarly, it is now widely held that two consenting adults "having casual sex" is morally acceptable. This has been voiced so adamantly that it is now accepted by society.

Today, the endless competition among network sponsors has driven advertisers to create commercials in which sex and the human body have become the dominant force used to catch and hold the attention of the viewer. Whether they are marketing cars, soft drinks, makeup, chewing gum or shampoo, the stereotypically perfect male and female models are seen in advertisements. The young people of America, who buy most of these products, are interested in sex, so what better way could there be to catch their attention than with half-naked bodies? The problem is that these commercials are also being seen by children who have not yet been "privileged" to have their sexual desires awakened. Because of such exposure, these interests are sparked early, and by the time they enter puberty, they have already learned about the mechanics of sex and are looking for someone with whom it can be experienced. They do not, however, understand all the dynamics affecting human sexuality.

Approximately sixty out of 100 movies released in a season will be rated "R." An "R" rating means that nudity, very strong language and violence will be present. An "R" rating also places an age limit on the viewing audience. The viewer must be seventeen years of age or older or he must be accompanied by an adult in order to attend. When the movie goes to the various cable networks, such as HBO, a preceding warning is announced to notify parents, but many parents ignore the warning and allow their young teenagers to watch the movies. Many theaters permit underage young people to attend R-rated movies as well.

Most of these movies are either "comedies," or "thrillers." The comedies usually depict high school or college-age teens with one or two main characters who are looking for sexual activity. The thrillers usually depict an evil being preying on numerous victims before it is killed in the end. The plots are shallow and they frequently depend heavily on sex, blood, and action to draw their audiences.

In the past, the final kiss at the end of the film was a highlight of many movies. Actors of earlier eras did not have access to the special effects and sexual freedoms which are utilized by actors of today. Instead of making movies better, this has simply made them more eventful. Our sexual "progress" can be seen on screens nationwide each movie season.

Pornography

Many modern movies are based on best-selling novels, which doesn't really say much for the novels that are being written today. Many of today's best-selling novelists tend to rely on occult-oriented fiction, sexual explicitness, and romantic-affair type adventures in order to entertain the reader.

From "soft-porn" publications like *Playboy,* which many call "art," to "hardcore" publications such as *Swedish Erotica,* pornography takes on many forms by exhibiting itself in magazines, books, and videos.

Child pornography or "kiddie porn" is a major underground favorite. Many will claim this is untrue, but the facts speak loudly. Full-color photographs of penetration, orgasm, oral sex, anal sex, bestiality, homosexuality, and other such perversions can be found in every "adult" bookstore in the country. A complete line of novels is also available. These novels depict lustful, sado-masochistic orgies, exotic new experiments with an array of instruments and prosthetics and vulgar perversions.

All of this creates what is commonly called "the sexual revolution." But what are the results of this "revolution"?

Homosexuality

The homosexual movement has grown to such an extent that "gays" are protesting for rights and requesting special attention in a voice so strong that our government is being forced to listen. Many adolescents today are being told they are gay, and that they were born that way. When a boy tells a psychologist he isn't interested in girls, the psychologist probes for "signs" of homosexual desires. The presumption is that all teenagers must be sexually active or yearnful, or they are emotionally and socially repressed. Adolescents who are told they are gay, are then told nothing is wrong with being the way they are, and they should accept it. They are also told God doesn't condemn them for being that way because He made them.

Most homosexuals don't consider God to be a part of their lives, however, there are a number who will declare themselves to be Christians. They argue that a loving God will honor love between two people and not object to sex simply because two people are of the same gender. When confronted with Bible verses condemning homosexuality as a sin, they reply that those verses were translated by biased linguists who condemned homosexuality, and that God did not mean that it is wrong originally.

These arguments are pallid when contrasted with evidence of scriptural authenticity. Simply put, as Dr. Roy Blizzard has said, "God made Adam and Eve. He didn't make Adam and Ebert." The Bible strictly forbids adultery and homosexuality in no uncertain terms.

Teenage Pregnancies

Another result of America's sexual revolution is the increased problems surrounding teenage pregnancies. One baby out of every five is born to a teenage mother. Nationally it is estimated that eight out of ten girls who become pregnant at seventeen years of age or younger never finish high school. Six hundred thousand (600,000) babies are born to teenage mothers each year and 500,000 babies are killed through abortion every year. Researchers today maintain that well over one million unwed teenage girls become pregnant each year. As a good friend once told me, "The question today is not, 'Should I get an abortion?' but rather, 'Why am I even pregnant in the first place?' "

AIDS and STDs

Today's outbreak of AIDS has caused a paranoia to sweep across our country. The disease is, for the most part, sexually transmitted or transmitted intravenously among drug addicts using contaminated needles. The disease is thought to have begun in the green monkey of Africa. How it got from the monkey to humans is still unknown. Some believe it may have been transmitted by eating the monkeys, while others believe it was transmitted through bestiality. It is known, however, that homosexual tourists brought it to America.

AIDS remained a "homosexual disease" for many years, but as time passed, bisexuals transmitted the disease to heterosexuals. Today, it is simply a sexual disease — a fatal virus. Those who have casual sex with various partners run a high risk of contracting it.

The Bible records the tale of two cities that were as sexually promiscuous as America is today: Sodom and Gomorrah. God destroyed these cities because of their sin. AIDS is not God's judgment on America. It is a result of sin, and in this plague we can hear God's plea for His people to stop sinning. He loves us, and He has warned us about the wages of sin through His Word. Instead of stopping, society has begun a "safe sex" campaign. Society is not willing to turn from a sin that could very well destroy it. Instead, they look for a way to protect people who persist in their sin.

Relationships

Within our society, one out of every two marriages ends in divorce. Within the Christian Church, however, only one out of every 3,000 marriages ends in divorce. Why is there such a difference? It is because the Church teaches sexuality from a spiritual perspective. A spouse is a companion, a friend, and not just a sexual partner. He or she is someone to love and cherish, not an object to possess and use.

People who base their relationship on sex, or begin their relationship with sex will fall. Their marriage will crumble on that foundation. Sex is not a foundation, sex is not love. Sex is the joining of two people to produce the greatest miracle after salvation — the inception of a human life. Sex is a result of love, a gift to be used and enjoyed by two people who have chosen to spend their lives together.

When God created Adam and Eve, He gave them a gift. He made reproduction enjoyable and desirable. Instead of being driven by animal instincts (like some agnostics will claim), we are given the freedom of choice and the capacity for intimacy. Sex for humans is much more than reproduction. Sex is the ultimate experience of knowing the person you have chosen as your mate and in that right perspective it is neither sinful nor ugly nor immoral. It is beautiful.

When a girl loses her virginity to a boy she barely knows, it strips away the tenderness and specialness of the moment when she will give herself to her husband. Because humans are not driven by uncontrollable instincts, we are expected to exercise deep responsibility with the gifts we have been given.

By not teaching the spiritual aspects of sex to the teenager, our society has given a "loaded gun" to a child who has never seen one before, and told that child to do whatever he wants with it. The results are always disastrous.

The human body is a thing of awesome beauty to a person in love. To look upon one's husband or wife is like finding a deer drinking at a silent stream before a sunrise. The human spirit finds peace and awe at beholding such beauty and tenderness. That is the way God meant for the body to be looked upon. It is the birthright of every person in creation to be joined wholly and purely to a husband or wife in Christ. Today, that birthright is being stolen.

Occultism and Sexual Perversions

Perverted sex has always been a part of occultism. From the earliest accounts of Babel to Sodom, sex has dominated occult worship practices. Temple prostitutes, both men and women, were common in all pagan cultures; the act of sex was a ceremonial uniting of the worshiper to the deity.

Man's nature causes him to seek to destroy that which he does not understand and society has destroyed the specialness God ordained for sex by not understanding it. Society has perverted and stripped away the beauty of the body and the miracle of love through sex. We can bring back these aspects only by returning to God's ideals.

Boys need to understand that girls are not made for their sexual fulfillment or for their lustful eyes. They were created to be man's companion and should be treated with respect and tenderness. Girls are sexually aroused by a touch, so pay attention to where your hands are and keep them where they belong. A very good rule to follow when dating: Treat your girlfriend as if she were a princess, for she is the King's child.

Girls need to understand that boys are not prizes to claim in front of their friends. They are people with emotions, and feelings. Society has placed a responsibility on boys to be successful, strong and dominant. Boys are aroused by a look, so be careful how you dress. Suggestive clothing is not only improper and detrimental to a girl's beauty, it can cause problems that are easily avoided. Young ladies may often be forced to be the strong ones in a relationship because of how society has placed the male figure. This is not right, but it is nonetheless true. Don't be afraid to say "no," girls. If your boyfriend breaks up with you because you refuse to "fool around" even moderately, he really didn't love you in the first place.

It's not easy. Sexual temptation is hard to overcome once it establishes a hold on a person. Before that hold is established, or after it is broken, it is one of the easiest temptations to defeat. Hold on. Hold fast to your ideals. Others will respect you, and when they don't, they will envy you for your victory when they fall. Today sex is a problem, not an answer. Sex was made for marriage and when it is used before marriage, it may require a payment you cannot afford to make. Hold fast to your ideals, and claim your victory.

10
Music

Rock and Roll

A number of books have been written on the subject of rock music. Some of these are supportive, others not so supportive, and many prominent Christian leaders disagree on the subject of rock music. Very few uphold rock music, as if to say the style itself is evil.

Music plays a big role in the teenager's life and it deserves to be recognized as such. Bob Pittman, the driving force behind MTV, has said, "The strongest appeal you can make is emotional. . . If you can get their emotions going (make them) forget their logic, then you've got 'em." Keeping that in mind, let's look at the subject rationally.

In 1966 John Lennon was recorded in *Newsweek* as having said, "Christianity will go. It will go. It will vanish and shrink. I needn't argue about it. I'm right, right and will be proved right. We are more popular than Jesus now. I don't know which will go first, rock 'n' roll or Christianity."

Today, it would seem that rock music and Christianity are in competition. Teenagers are being told, "Rock music or Jesus, *now choose.*" This really causes problems for teenagers. Al Manconi said it very well in *Media Update,* "These evangelists may be men of God . . . but when it comes to music, they are off base."

Most teenagers don't care for other types of music. This is why there is such turmoil associated with the idea of giving up rock music. For the teenager it literally means giving up all music, and that is not easy for them even to consider, much less to do.

Those who speak out against all forms of rock music seem to believe they can look into the spirit of a young Christian and determine what is and what is not spiritually edifying. By doing so, they are projecting their tastes and limits on God. Looking at rock music as it is today, we need not really ask why they react this way.

The entertainment world, especially rock music, is controlled by money and prestige. Blackie Lawless of W.A.S.P. said in *Hit Parader,* "Rock and roll is a business to me." Most musicians do what they do for money, regardless of the influences their songs and actions may have upon others.

Teenagers idolize the stars of rock bands, and the members of the bands are quite aware of this. A person who has no regard for the lives he or she influences should not be given such a position. There is a deep responsibility that comes with fame, and a person controlled by money is nothing more than a puppet, with no way to justify his actions.

Mike Bloodgood said in *Faces,* "I'm personally really sick of these guys saying they have no responsibility to their audience."

Satanic Overtones

Today, drugs, sexual and satanic overtones are very dominant in rock music. Motley Crue sings of "Girls, Girls, Girls," and their video documents a night of fun at a strip bar. Ozzy Ozbourne sings of "The Ultimate Sin." Keeping a rational view on things, these three subjects, because they are so dominant in our society, are the most logical things to be singing about if you are a money-hungry musician.

Songs are filled with sexual, violent, and demonic references, which are further promoted by the groups' videos. It really doesn't matter if the musicians believe in the things they sing about, what really matters is the effect these things have on the listener, and whether or not the listener believes in these things.

Probably the most shocking group since KISS removed their makeup and Ozzy calmed down with his family is W.A.S.P. Singer Blackie Lawless said, "Everyone needs some sort of gimmick . . . our stuff is entertainment, pure and simple. It's designed to shock people, but it's never demonic." And yet, Blackie often drinks what appears to be blood from a human skull on stage, and has tied a naked girl to a rack and pretended to slit her throat. Is this entertainment? Are we really to believe this is not having any effect on young teenagers who watch it?

Before I became a Christian and before the media became interested in the Ninja craze, I was very involved in the martial arts. When the Ninja movies came to cable, I would record them on our

VCR and a young cousin of mine often begged me to watch them. When the movie would finish, the child would get up from his place before the television and run through the house doing "Karate kicks" and beating up the dog. After a few such episodes, I would no longer allow him to watch those movies because of their influence on him.

Violence

The same type of things can be seen when concerts let out. Teenagers hyped by the energy of the groups often break things, fight, use spray paint on everything they see, etc. The satanic influence is definitely there. Stryper's Michael Sweet said it very well in *Hit Parader.* "There's absolutely no reason why sex and violence have to play such a big part in some bands' presentations."

Some bands are not violent at all. In fact, for the most part, only the heavy metal bands have that reputation. Most bands are energetic and often dynamic with stage shows, complete with smoke and lazers. Still, these bands have just as much influence over their fans as do the heavy metal bands. What is it these other bands are representing to the teenagers?

The lyrical content of songs is the most influential part of the group's production. Radio is still the most dominant outreach in music. There's not a heartbroken teenager around who will say that lyrics don't have any effect on the listener. So what is it that the groups are saying? Sadly enough, not too much of it is that good.

The Influence of the Lyrics

Starship, when they released 'Long John Silver' (they were still Jefferson Airplane at the time) spoke of Jesus Christ as a bastard who had an affair with Mary Magdalene. Today, they sing about "love." That's what most of the groups are singing about, love, or so it would appear. Most of the time these groups are still singing about sex. Steve Camp said in *Calendar,* "I realized that being on the edge for these kids is not just rock and roll. Its the lyrics that they're hooking into."

When looking at a song rationally, with just its lyrics, no music, the song takes on new meaning, a truer meaning. Music tends to bring about emotions which dull the ability to consider things rationally. For instance, "Don't Fear the Reaper" is a mellow and a pretty song that speaks of death. The lyrics being sung might even be interpreted by a Christian as acceptable, but when the music is gone and the lyrics are read, the true meaning of the song is revealed as nothing but the call and adoration for a Christless, "romantic" death.

So, for the most part, the Christian leaders who speak against rock music are correct in doing so. However, simply because it is rock music, does not make it bad.

The Beat

Many maintain that the beat in rock music calls up demons and causes rebellion and other problems in the lives of young people. However, any beat can be used as a part of satanic ritual and unless it is used along with the other elements of witchcraft, it's not going to evoke a demonic response. No occultic book particularly mentions one form of music as being better or worse than another, and there is no biblical reference for types of music being below or above others.

Music was created by God. Satan did not create music. Satan has never created anything. *He only perverts that which God creates for His purpose.* Music can be both good and evil. The way it is used and the reasons behind it determine its effects. Steve Whitaker of Barren Cross said in *Faces,* "You are either for God or you're not."

Jesus is not a novelty. He is the Lord and Savior of our lives. Punk rock singer Pattie Smith, in her poem 'Oath' says, "Jesus died for somebody's sins — but not mine. My sins are my own, they belong to me." Don't be foolish. Robert Sweet of the Christian group Stryper said in *Concert Shots,* "If my old life had something better to offer, why would I be doing this?"

How to Choose What Music to Listen to

When you choose your music, do so with reason instead of emotion. Here are four things to look at when making decisions about musicians and bands:
1. What do the lyrics say?
2. What kind of life-styles have the musicians chosen?
3. What do the graphics on the album cover indicate?

4. What are the goals of the songs and performers?

When you make your decisions, keep in mind who Jesus is to you. When choosing from Christian labels, remember the same four things, and compare the Christian musicians' life-styles to the secular musicians' life-styles. Which would you approve of if you were a parent? This comparison can be valuable when people tell you your music is wrong.

11
SUICIDE

Of all the problems we face, suicide is, in many ways, the most difficult and alarming. It is a result of other problems and it is a problem in itself.

Causes

Teens who kill themselves believe it is an answer to life's pain. Dr. Mary Griffin, a former neurologist, now a psychiatrist, has said, "(Teenagers) are killing the hopelessness. They really don't mean to be killing themselves. The act of suicide says, 'The only way I can see to be helped is to kill myself. Please find another answer for me.' "

Over the past thirty years, suicide rates for adults have remained static, but the suicide rate for teenagers began to climb in the mid 1950's, and had tripled by 1978. In 1950 the suicide rate for people, aged fifteen to twenty-four was 4.9 per 100,000. Today, the national average is 9.2 per 100,000. Nine teens out of every 100,000 are killing themselves!

According to the National Institute of Mental Health, as many as fifteen children kill themselves every day. That's 5,000 teenagers each year, with another 500,000 attempting suicide. Experts also observe that two-thirds of those who attempt to commit suicide will try again at least once.

Why are many youths so eager to kill themselves? Experts have come up with hundreds of reasons, but these reasons, they also agree, are common in all teenagers everywhere. So they maintain that they really don't know the answer to the question.

So why are the youth of America so eager to kill themselves? The answer is both complex and simple. Teenagers are searching. They are seeking truth, a future, love, and life. Many cannot find that for which they are so desperately searching. Everywhere they look they find death, pain, hopelesness, and darkness, and so, they give up. They can't find a place where they fit in. They are told God doesn't exist. Death is it; there is no afterlife. Many have believed that a nuclear war will occur within their lifetime, and many other things drive them into hopelessness. They search for peace, but can't find it, and death becomes the only answer.

Simply put, God created every person with an empty spot inside them that only He can fill, and He gave man the insatiable desire to fill that spot so man will seek Him out. When the teenager finds he cannot fill this void with the things he has found, and the desire for peace becomes an obsession with no answer, he gives up, and turns to the only answer he can see — death.

When that emptiness is filled with the love of Jesus Christ, the desire for death as an escape from pain will vanish because the pain itself is gone. Then comes a purpose for life, a reason to live, hope in the future, peace and eminent love.

There are certain signs to look for to ascertain if someone is considering suicide. These signs are almost always present in the lives of people who are contemplating suicide. The existence of these signs does not necessarily indicate suicidal thinking, but they certainly may be such indicators. You may be able to see the signs when others may not. Don't ignore the problem. Tell someone about it and do what you can to help.

The Signs

Many of the symptoms of suicidal feelings are similar to those of depression, according to the American Academy of Child Psychiatry. The academy recommends that if one or more of the following warning signs occurs, someone should talk to the person, and if they persist, professional help should be sought:

— Changes in eating and sleeping habits.
— Withdrawal from friends, family and regular activities.
— Violent or rebellious behavior.
— Running away.
— Drug or alcohol abuse.
— Unusual neglect of personal appearance.
— Drastic change in personality.
— Persistent boredom, difficulty concentrating, or a decline in the quality of schoolwork.

— Frequent complaints about physical symptoms that are often related to emotions, such as stomachaches, headaches, or fatigue.
— Loss of interest in previously pleasurable activities.
— Inability to tolerate praise or rewards.

In addition, a teenager who is contemplating suicide may complain of being "rotten inside," give verbal hints (i.e. "I won't be a problem for much longer" or "It'll all be over soon."), or put his or her affairs in order. He or she may give away favorite possessions; or become suddenly cheerful, without salvation, after a period of depression.

The question will probably come up in the suicidal person's thoughts. "Will I go to heaven or will I go to hell?" The answer, of course, can be known only by God, for only He knows the true hearts of people. For the most part, however, that answer will be hell, not because of the sin of suicide, but because of the fact that the person has not accepted Jesus Christ as his Savior.

How to Help

You can show someone who may be considering suicide the answer to his questions by showing him how to fill the empty place within him. Just show him that you care about him. Tell him you love him. The words "I love you" have more effect than you may think. Tell him, "I love you, because Jesus loves you."

Take him and show him the beauty of the world. Show him the sky and the trees and the small animals. Tell him that Jesus expresses His love for him in all these things, so he will come to Him. Let him know how much Jesus loves him, and that He has a purpose for his life.

12

Questions I Am Most Frequently Asked

I am not qualified to be an "answer man" of any sort but I can speak from my personal experience. I have been a Christian for only four years, and although I have studied quite a lot, I realize there are so many more things about life that I do not know in contrast with the things I do know.

Nonetheless, people have gone to great lengths to seek me out in order to ask me questions on a wide range of subjects. I sometimes feel that pastors should be answering these questions rather than myself — a twenty-year-old, death-row inmate. In spite of these feelings, I always try to answer each question to the best of my ability.

I hope no one will use these answers as the voice of authority because I give only my own opinions. (If people want to quote my work, I hope it will be my poetry.) My greatest desire is that my answers and opinions given in response to the following questions will excite readers with Christian passion, motivation and even the anger that moves me to reach out beyond the obstacles that surround me.

Why does God let evil things happen?

This question comes in many forms. Numerous times I have read letters by and about people who are angry with God because "He let someone die" in a car wreck, or through suicide, or as a result of some disease. This question makes me more frustrated (at people) than any other question I am asked. (How can people blame God for everything bad that happens?) I too once asked this question, when I was thirteen, and it led me to seek my answers in Satan.

Why does evil exist in the first place? Because it is necessary. God created evil for a purpose, and He perpetuates it for a purpose. (See Isaiah 45:7; 37:36; 54:16). Jewish rabbis have used a simile to describe the desire for a total absence of evil. They have pointed out that it is like a man carrying a lamp in broad daylight. What's the point? A lamp is needed only in darkness. Evil exists because without it mankind would not have the ability to choose between good and evil. Without the ability to choose, man has no freedom of choice, and without freedom of choice, man is nothing more than a robot, or even a slave.

God created the angels to do nothing but serve Him. Man was created in the image of God, and in Eden God planted the tree of knowledge of good and evil. Man chose to disobey God by eating of the fruit of that tree, and we continue to reap the fruits of that disobedience even now.

Today people continually want God to turn them into robot-like creatures. People want God to stop the drunken driver, for example, before that driver injures or kills someone. They get mad at God when that driver slams into a tree or kills an innocent person.

The current issues surrounding AIDS are a case in point as well. The HIV virus is a direct result of sexual immorality. Whatever its origins, it came to people as a result of immoral behavior. God has forbidden homosexuality, drug abuse and fornication. Although certain people have contracted the disease through blood transfusions, these unfortunate individuals are victims of man's irresponsibility and immorality. The important thing to remember is that AIDS is mankind's fault, not God's!

Mankind frequently refuses to accept responsibility for his actions. From the very beginning, when Adam blamed Eve and Eve blamed the serpent, we have sought excuses for our mistakes and failures. Perhaps when we begin accepting the responsibility that life gives us, we will understand where to place the blame for our planet's problems and we will then return to serving the Creator.

Are demons real?

Most Christians don't ask this question. There are plenty of Scripture references which clearly point out the existence of demons. There are some so-called Christians, however, who find it difficult in today's technological age to believe in the existence of demons. they accredit a belief in demons to the same ignorance that led to the witch trials in Salem. (The only problem is that the witches in Salem went free while they manipulated the community to kill innocent people.)

Demons *are* real. They exist in many forms and under many names. Beneath every idol worshiped in India there is a demon. Every detached spirit heard in a seance is a demon. The promoters of atheism and New Age spiritism are demons. The source of racial hatred and bigotry is demons. The promoters of fanatical Christian theologies and cult beliefs are demons. The forces behind white and black magic, and satanism are all demons.

Demons are spirit creatures who are subject to the power of God. Christians have authority over demons by the name of Jesus. But few Christians exercise their God-given authority. Because of Hollywood movies like "The Exorcist" and "Ghoulies," demons have been glorified and they have been given much more power than they deserve.

Ministers spend far too much time trying to cast out demons; they seek demons' names, question how long they've been in a person and other such irrelevant matters. Ministers who understand their place of authority don't have to spend time playing games with demons. The late Smith Wigglesworth spoke once to demons, and the creatures fled. He did not permit them to speak or to disobey. It is this type of authority that Christians should be exercising.

Demons do exist, but they're not a serious problem. Demons receive far too much attention today.

Can demons possess Christians?

Ultimately the answer is a simple no. But problems arise from that simple answer. People who are supposed to be Christians continue to do things that are very un-Christian. And then there are the many cults who maintain they are Christian — some even include Jesus as their Savior. There have been true, Spirit-filled Christians who have turned away from God and have become satanists. If their profession was true, there have been Christians who have been possessed by demons.

This should clear the confusion: Salvation is not a one-time decision. Being a Christian is a daily way of life. It is a life style of daily decisions, to serve God or not to serve God. It is simply a matter of daily choice, and as long as a person *wants* to be a Christian, he or she *will* be.

As long as a person is serving God, no demon can possess him. It is when people begin turning away from God, when they begin letting greed, hatred, pride, or other ungodly ideals enter their lives, that oppressive demons begin taking authority over them and then possess them. No demon can possess a Christian against that Christian's will.

Is there a network of satanist organizations in the world?

Many people who work in ministries that deal with the occult believe there is. Here is why. Rumors and occurrences that are often quite bizarre drift in simultaneously from different parts of the country. Before Halloween of 1989, for example, ministries across the country were hearing rumors that contracts had been put out for blonde-haired, blue-eyed children. Ritualistically abused children have told almost identical stories from opposite sides of the country. These things seem to point to organization and planning.

People who do not have much experience with the occult often cannot believe such a network exists. Their reasoning is logical. There is no proof. We don't have reports from people who have ever talked to someone who has been a part of such an organization. These points are true. There is no proof. However, that does not negate the network's existence.

The secret group of Nazis known as the Odessa which formed after World War II existed for a long time before it was discovered. It is also a fact that generational satanists were in America for 200 years before it was even known that such families existed. It is very possible that these families have established themselves in the world's societies and are working together.

It *is* known that some of the psychotic killers who have been responsible for dozens of murders have been members of satanic groups, and some have acted out their crimes under orders from these groups.

Perhaps a true organized network of occultism does not exist. It is possible that the apparent simultaneous tendencies of separate groups are inspired not by human organization, but in accordance with a spiritual plan. Maybe the dark powers these groups serve lead them to synchronize their evil deeds.

Whatever the truth is, it remains a fact that there are many satanist organizations, some centuries old, which have common goals and diligently work toward them daily, and each of them are sworn enemies of all Christians.

How do I get out of satanism?

I have worked with many people who have been eager to escape Satan's web. I have also worked with a few who are not so eager to escape. Getting into satanism is easy. Getting out is not.

The first problem many people encounter when they attempt to flee from a coven is that the people they had formerly called their friends turn against them. Satanism is like the Mafia, you don't simply quit! Coven members often look after their own. They protect each other, provide for each other, and act as if they are a family. Orgies are very common in covens. When this "family" relationship is forsaken, coven members turn on the person who is seeking a way out. They become like rabid dogs. There is no limit to the cruelty often displayed toward those who have "betrayed" or "forsaken" the coven.

I have worked with some minor cases where coven members brought cocaine to a girl who was trying to kick her addiction. They would bring her only enough to feed her addiction and make her want more, leaving it in her window each night. Another girl found her dog hanging by a wire on her front porch with a note written in the pet's blood: "Come back, or you will be next!"

I have also worked with major cases where people have been tortured and where coven members have employed hit men to murder those who were trying to flee.

Because of this, a change in environment is almost always necessary for someone who wants to get out of the occult. I always make people do two things when they come to me seeking a way out of satanism. Number 1 — They must destroy all the occult-related books, jewelry, and other paraphernalia they possess. Books should be burnt and metal and jewelry should be hammered, then thrown away.

If a person refuses to do these things, I will not help them. These acts are symbolic gestures that show true repentance and a genuine desire to get out. It is at this point that many will back out. Occult materials are valuable (in a monetary sense), and people often want to keep or sell them. Such individuals are not ready to commit themselves to the task of getting out.

Number 2 — I lead them to accept Jesus as their Savior and to commit to changing their life style. Words are easy. Salvation is not an emotional moment which has little effect on an individual. Salvation entails a change in behavior, and I try to act as a guide for those I disciple. For the first month I am usually a little rough. I demand that a church be found, that the Bible be read, that all contact with coven members be cut, that black metal music is no longer allowed, etc. If a person eagerly *tries* to accept these changes — *tries* (I don't demand miracles), then I know he is sincere. If he doesn't, then he is not.

This rigid system was developed by trial and error over the past two years, and though it may seem a bit legalistic, it works. The one common problem is the lack of help we receive from local churches and ministers.

When a person sincerely tries to break away from occultism, he often finds himself in a very lonely world. Former friends are now enemies, and there is seldom anyone to take their place.

It is impossible to separate the love of God from the love of man. People escaping satanism will never learn of God's love for them unless the Church shows her love for them. Christians need to be far more conscious of the pain in the world than they are now. Sometimes people return to the occult because of the treatment they receive from Christians — they feel more loved by the coven members.

Can God forgive me?

It is alarming how many people ask this question. I honestly think few people have been as bad as I have, and yet this is a question I never contemplated. God's forgiveness was clear to me, and, in fact, it was the forgiveness of God that demanded that I forgive myself.

The Bible is clear in many places concerning God's forgiveness:

> Again, when the wicked man turneth away from his wickedness that he hath committed, and doeth that which is lawful and right, he shall save his soul alive. Because he considereth, and turneth away from all his transgressions that he hath committed, he shall surely live, he shall not die.
> (Ezek. 18:27-28)

> Come now, and let us reason together, saith the Lord; though your sins be as scarlet, they shall be as white as snow; though they be red like crimson, they shall be as wool.
> (Isa. 1:18)

There are no conditions in God's forgiveness except repentance. God's forgiveness is without measure, and that is something that must be accepted simply. The Jews obeyed the law that Moses gave to them without question.

> Observe and hear all these words [commands]
> . . . (Deut. 12:28)

Jewish rabbis taught that they obeyed before they heard why. They accepted the Torah simply because God gave it to them regardless of whether they understood the reasons or not. So, too, must we obey and accept God's forgiveness. To not do so is to say, "The death of Jesus was not enough." That is blasphemy.

And when we fail, we get up and try again:

> For though a righteous man falls seven times,
> he rises again.
>
> (Prov. 24:16)

What can I do to help?

This question is usually directed at me, but I seldom need much help. The Lord looks after His children, including me. However, I think if people would ask this question more often to everyone around them, this book would not be needed today.

Everywhere in the world there are people who are in need and Christians often are really a lazy group of individuals. We spend so much time playing "Bless me" that we ignore the needs of the hungry, the homeless, the sick, the lonely, and the hurting.

Occultism today would not be the growing problem it is if the Church was as diligent to her work as the occultists are to theirs. We spend so much time doing nothing and waste so much time in misdirected energy that we *let* the enemy beat us.

Responsibility is a call word in this book. It is time for Christians either to begin accepting the responsibility of their title or to begin calling themselves by another name. In short, either walk what you talk, or change what you're saying.

Christians need to see the problems around us — the suicide, the divorce, the occultism, the pain — and we need to ask, "What can I do to help?"

Precious people of God, don't tell them Jesus loves them until you're ready to love them too.

PART V

The Way to Freedom

Stand fast therefore in the liberty wherewith Christ hath made us free, and be not entangled again with the yoke of bondage"

(Galatians 5:1).

13

Freedom —
The False and the True

The Biggest Influence on Teenagers Today

Teenagers are faced with more problems and responsibilities today than any generation in history has known. The average sixteen-year-old student has probably known someone who is involved in the occult, been around drugs first-hand, heard about someone killing himself, and at the very least, seriously considered having sex, if not actually doing so. At the same time, he is having to focus on the transition from childhood to adulthood. Teens are faced with numerous temptations and problems that require mature, life-changing decisions. However, we're not being taught skills that help us deal with these problems and make these decisions.

The biggest influence on teenagers is the society in which they live, and that society has little apparent concern about the individuals it affects. Society is controlled by money, statistics, and competition. Our government has stopped looking at people. It looks instead at paper and numbers, not realizing that each statistical number represents the life of a human being.

The Price of Peace

Wars very seldom end in victory. Politicians making decisions for negotiations, and soldiers tired of fighting, are tempted to give in to the ideals of the enemy and compromise to end the bloodshed.

However, as soon as the wounds heal and the violence is forgotten, the enemy ideals bring hated oppression to the ones who agree to them, and the spirit of rebellion arises, causing a renewed war. As soon as the soldiers tire of fighting, they will once again give in and the cycle will begin anew. Unless, that is, determination overcomes fatigue, and will power overcomes stress. Then, the fighting will continue until a victory is claimed, and with that victory, peace.

There is a price for peace, a price that every veteran knows, a price that seems to have been forgotten by our society. The price is blood. Peace is not claimed except through bloodshed, and it is not kept except by holding fast to the ideals that brought the victory. Every person and every country that leaves their ideals behind and allows change and compromise to infiltrate their foundation, will fall. Every person and every country that doesn't have a sound foundation to begin with, will also fall.

Today, America and several other nations seem to be allowing that very thing to happen. It has been said that no enemy could ever defeat this nation by attacking her shores. If America should ever fall, it would come from within. Today America appears to be on the verge of failure.

America's Moral Failure

The evidence of this failure is all around and yet people do not see it. In an effort to balance America's budget, proposals have been made to issue a call for a constitutional convention, which will literally alter America's foundation. Also, in 1976, 104 congressmen met to sign a document called the Declaration of Interdependence. This document is a declaration that a one-world government is needed, no matter what the cost.

It states, "We affirm that the resources of the globe . . . are the heritage of no one nation or generation, but of all peoples, nations, and of posterity, and that our deepest obligation is to transmit to that posterity a planet richer in material bounty . . . narrow notions of national sovereignty must not be permitted to curtail that obligation." This declaration may have a great effect upon the changes in the constitution. Although the ideals of this declaration are well-intended, it could very easily lead democratic nations to adopt a socialistic/communistic set of ideals in an effort to "transmit the resources of the globe to all people."

In 1960, Mrs. Madalyn Murray O'Hair won her famed battle with the Supreme Court. And, the First Amendment, which states, "Congress shall make no law respecting an establishment of religion, or prohibiting the free exercise thereof," was perverted so that today, Christians cannot legally pray in school. Mrs. O'Hair, in a mad protest of her ideal that there is no God, used her son as the tool and weapon to remove God from America's foundation.

The First Amendment was written by people who came to a new land in search of freedom from oppression. They came to America so they could freely worship as they wished. The amendment was written to keep the government from placing limits, standards, and rules upon that worship. It was *never* written to keep prayer and worship separate from the government. The foundation was altered, cracked, and the result is that today, most of America knows nothing of its true foundation, Jesus Christ.

The price of freedom and peace is blood, and the precious blood of Jesus has bought victory for the true Christian body. America's foundation was formed on that blood, but today that foundation cannot even be found in many circles. In the 1960's, the top problems in America's schools, according to a national survey, were: chewing gum in class, talking in class, running in the halls, pushing and cutting in lines, throwing spit balls, and inappropriate dress. Today the top problems in America's schools, according to the same survey, are: assault, murder, rape, pregnancy, drugs, suicide, and arson. Do people still argue that America has no real problems?

The Key to Restoration

America's foundation was the blood of Christ, and America's backbone, the family unit. When the foundation of a house cracks, the supporting structure begins to decay as well. Today, because Christ is forgotten, one out of every two marriages ends in divorce, thus the backbone or supporting structure of America has been shattered. School used to be the crutch when the backbone failed, but today the crutch is also broken. With no crutch, no backbone, and no foundation, how is America going to possibly stand and remain strong?

America can, and must, be restored and soon. She must return to her foundation and uphold the ideals of that foundation. The power to do that is not in the politicians, not in the government, not in the armies. The power to restore America is in its youth. The teens of today are the future of America. *You,* young person, are the one who can make a difference. *You* have the ability and power to change America.

Ancient Israel was the most awesome army and nation the world has ever known. They followed the Lord into battle, won victory after victory, and even their very name brought fear to their enemies. They were undefeated until they too began to compromise and turn away from God, and yet, each time they returned to the Lord, they rose once again in victory. Today Israel is the Christian body, the Church that has Jesus at its heart.

We must return to the old ideals and original foundation that the Church was birthed on. We are one nation under God, and once we return to that ideal, we must not allow any compromise to overcome our victory. As teenagers, we are the future. As Christians, we are God's army, following

Him into battle, and we have the responsibility of representing Him to the world.

Jesus said: "Not everyone that saith unto me, Lord, Lord, shall enter into the kingdom of heaven; but he that doeth the will of my Father which is in heaven" (Matt. 7:21)

As a Christian, a person is called to represent Jesus. We are called to represent Him as we would have Him do for us. No compromise, no exceptions, with a tenacity that can be laid at the Father's feet when all work is done. To live, work, fight, and die for Jesus Christ is what it means to be a true Christian.

Before a warrior can defend himself against an enemy, he must know something about that enemy, and be trained to fight. Each problem society has that affects us is an enemy to Christ. These problems are an enemy to you if you are a Christian warrior.

14

The Spiritual World

Contrary to the educated opinions of many well-respected psychologists around the world, the realm of the supernatural (the spiritual dimension, or spirit world) *does* exist. I have seen it and experienced it in a variety of ways. A multitude of unexplained phenomena give evidence of the existence of *something* beyond our rational ability to understand. Whether we are atheists, Christians, or satanists, we have to acknowledge the existence of the unknown.

To the atheist, who may rely on the science of psychology, the spiritual realm is nothing more than the untapped energies of the mind, or possibly, the mental imbalances of an imagination gone wild. Unexplained phenomena are disputed and called everything from lies to misunderstandings.

To the Christian, the spiritual realm is that dimension where time does not exist and where God, angels, and demons dwell. To the satanist, the spirit realm is first and foremost a source of much-sought power. It is that place where the substance of control and authority exist for them to harness; however, that takes work.

Spiritual Bridges

Between the physical and spiritual dimensions lies a vast chasm or void. A wall separates the two in order to prevent chaos. To the Christian, the sacrifice and blood of the Lord Jesus Christ provide a bridge from the physical realm into the spiritual world. It unites us with God and gives us a source of spiritual power. To the satanist or occultist or spiritist the bridge to the spiritual world is crossed with sacrifices, spells, rituals, or more commonly, various games and tools that are in vogue today.

Many tools for crossing spiritual bridges exist. They take on various forms, everything from games to jewelry. Ancient and somewhat complicated, these approaches are often overlooked as being harmless by the world's societies.

Within the spiritual realm there is the Creator and the adversary. Somewhere within the spiritual realm, also, we find the souls of those who have died. According to Judaism, the souls of those yet to be born may be found in the spiritual realm also. There are some who try to seek out the Creator by using occult tools and methods. They refuse to acknowledge biblical commandments that prohibit such acts, and instead, choose to believe what they want. Many more seek out the dead, and even more seek out the adversary (Satan) — if only in jest. Unwittingly, they call out to demons and spirits to give them power or knowledge, or they summon the souls of loved ones (or even strangers), to ease the pain of loneliness or to tell them secrets.

Rules of the Spiritual Realm

What rules apply to the spiritual realm? In the physical world there are rules (or laws) which govern existence. These rules govern gravity, energy, resistance, cause-and-effect, mass, weather, time, death, etc. In the same way, the spiritual realm has its own rules which govern its existence. These include rules of cause and effect, life and death, balance, love, and power.

The rule of power, or authority, establishes an order in the spiritual realm. It develops a chain of command that descends from the greatest power to the least. At the top of that order is the Creator, God Almighty. (There is a false teaching that God and Satan are of equal power. This doctrine has many different forms, from Jesus and Satan being rival brothers — with God as a neutral Father — to God and Satan being rival creators and Jesus, Buddha, Muhammad, Hitler, Crowley, etc., being their children. The truth is that there is only one Creator, Almighty God, and He is *the* Creator. He is the all-powerful One who inhabits eternity.) All that happens in the spiritual realm is subject to His power and will.

The Rule of Balance

Many people have asked, "If God is in control and He is good, why does He allow evil to exist?" This is best explained by a rule of balance.

The physical world is made up of opposites (up — down, predator — prey, action — reaction). Balance is an integral rule in both the physical and spiritual realms. In order to give man the freedom of choice (free will) which is the element that makes man unique, opposites from which to choose had to be established. Judaism teaches that God made man with both the inclination to do good and the inclination to do evil so he could choose between the two fairly.

All that God is became known as good. If man chooses to love God and to serve God, he also chooses to love and serve that which God represents. All that God is *not* became known as evil.

The entity called the adversary (Satan) represents all that is evil, creating necessary balance. If man was to choose *not* to serve God, he would then choose to love and to serve that which God was not, and in doing so, he would choose to serve evil and Satan. This has been God's law from the beginning.

God is like a great king. When the king makes laws they must apply to *everyone,* even the king himself. God will not infringe on the rights of choice which all mankind has. He will not make people serve Him. To do so would nullify the sacrifices many have made so that others might be free to serve Him. For God to violate His rules would not be fair to the prophets who were tortured and killed because they refused to do evil, or to the children who have endured teasing or exclusion because of their dedication to the Lord.

Love Is a Choice

Love means nothing unless it is chosen freely. Forced love is not real.

Let me use an example to illustrate this truth. A husband came home from work and said to his wife, "Hi, honey, do you love me?"

She said nothing.

He said, "Honey, I asked you if you love me."

Silence.

He took her by the throat, shoved her against the wall and yelled into her face, "I said, do you love me!"

She replied, "Yes, darling, I love you."

Such words mean nothing. They were forced. They are not real. *God will not force His people to love Him.*

Some contend that Satan is next to God. Those who maintain that Christ is not God, may place Jesus here. Others will say the Archangel Michael is next in the chain of command. The important point, however, is not "who is below God?" God *is* on top. This is an absolute truth. It can be scripturally demonstrated that the angels are below God. Satan and his demons are also subject to God.

Life and Death

The next rules are those of life and death. The spiritual rules of life and death are much different from those of the physical realm. In a realm where time cannot reach, eternity is the only measurement.

Scientists believe the time barrier is beyond the speed of light. If we could go faster than 186,000 miles per second, time would cease to exist. God existed before light did. He existed in the spiritual world where time does not apply.

Death in the physical world is the passage of the soul into the spiritual realm, and once that happens, there is no passing from the spiritual realm. There, life and death are determined by the presence or absence of God, who is the source of all life. The soul dwells forever with the forces it adhered itself to in life. No evil exists where God rules.

As evil is darkness and God is light, evil cannot withstand the presence of God. Evil is alien and opposite to God's very nature. Those who choose to serve Satan in the physical life will confront God only once — at the time of personal judgment. They will then enter into the eternal death of damnation in hell (the lake of fire).

The Rule of Choice

The existence of hell is the result of the rule of balance that we mentioned earlier. Heaven — a place where all that God *is* dwells, could not exist unless there was also a place where all that God is *not* dwells also. People *choose* hell by choosing to live away from the presence of the Lord.

God forces himself on no one (because of the rule of choice), and those who hate God or simply do not desire to draw close to Him, choose instead to live their lives by their own rules away from God's presence, in hell. Since hell is the absolute absence of all that God is, there is darkness (God is light), there is hatred (God is love), there is pain (God is the healer), there is anguish and sorrow (God is joy).

God sends no one to hell arbitrarily. We *choose* to go to hell by choosing to live in service to evil. There are only two choices, good or evil, God or Satan; and eternity is spent in the presence of the choices we make in this physical life. It is in this earthly life that the ultimate choice for life or death is made. And there are no second chances, no multiple lives to work it out. We have only one chance and only two choices: God or Satan.

Biblical Foundations

Many people refuse to acknowledge the foundations God has provided for man to build his life upon. The Bible is often ridiculed, its teachings are compromised, and people choose to follow their own ways in life, thinking God will not *really* mind.

Think about this before reading on: In every sport, in every job, in every home, there are certain rules. What football coach would keep a player who refused to run the plays he was told to run? What baseball coach would keep a player who always purposely threw the ball to the wrong teammate? What basketball coach *could* keep a player who refused to dribble the ball because carrying it was easier? What parent could tolerate a child who continuously disobeyed every request or household rule? In all these things we would think it absurd and foolishly rebellious to disregard the rules because we want to do it our own way. Why then do we think we can so easily disregard the rules God has established?

Some people do not trust the Bible. They think it is full of mistakes. If Christians, Buddhists, Muslims, or anyone (atheists in particular), could find a major flaw in the Bible, would they not take time to make sure that flaw was well known every time they spoke to people?

God has laid out His will for us in the Bible. Christianity, having its roots in Judaism, is the only religion that maintains there is only *one* way to the Lord: through Jesus Christ.

"Jesus saith unto him, I am the way, the truth, and the life: no man cometh unto the Father, but by me" (John 14:6). This single statement separates Christianity from all other religions. In considering this statement of Jesus we realize it is either a lie that makes all other Christian rules bogus, or it is the truth. The evidence to support His claim is seen in changed lives. (Christianity is the number-one rehabilitative influence in America's prisons; it is the number-one, marriage-saving factor in America's homes; and it is the number-one motivator for excellence in America's youth). The Bible's continuing survival in a world of enemies who are eager to disprove it, gives much credence to the acknowledgment of Christianity's *truth*.

If Christianity is indeed the true and only way to God, through Jesus Christ, then the Bible's rules forbidding witchcraft, sorcery, fortune telling, speaking to the dead, etc. must be true as well.

The Power of Prayer

Nothing happens in the spiritual realm of and by itself. Sometimes things happen for no apparent reason. The wind may blow a tower over, killing someone, or a car may hit someone because of faulty brakes.

Nothing like that ever happens in the spiritual world. There are no accidents in the spiritual realm. Everything that happens does so by the will of someone. That someone may be God, it may be Satan, or it may be human.

Prayers move both God and Satan. A man prays for forgiveness for the things he has done wrong in his life, and God answers his prayer with the peace of salvation. The cause is prayer. The effect is God moving with the spirit of forgiveness.

On the other hand, a man may pray for power to destroy an enemy while making a sacrifice to Satan. His prayer is answered with a burning hatred so consuming that he takes a gun and murders his enemy. The cause is prayer and sacrifice. The effect is power in the form of hatred.

These are elementary examples, but their simple structure is the basis of how things work in the spiritual world. In both examples, someone's will caused the resulting conditions. This is a constant in the spiritual realm. The will to obey, the will to rebel, the will to submit, the will to be tenacious, are all catalysts for things happening in the spiritual realm. And the things that happen there, *always affect the physical world.*

Individual choices to rebel against God cause things to happen in the spiritual realm. In so doing, the individual crosses bridges to the dark side, and the influence of evil affects the life of the person in rebellion.

The same thing happens when choices are made to rebel against Satan. Bridges are crossed to God.

Every person on earth has the opportunity (free will) to choose the path that his or her life will take. The rules of the spiritual realm cannot be ignored or broken. Those who rebel against God and choose to ignore His ways, will end up in an eternity away from Him.

15

A Word to Parents and Teenagers

"An ounce of prevention equals a pound of cure"? Everyone has heard this proverb, and it certainly applies to the topics of this book. The way to prevention is found in positive, open relationships based on honest communication and trust. Parents and teenagers who have such good relationships seldom have to worry about satanism, occultism, drugs, suicide, etc. invading their homes.

No Magic Formulas

Life provides us with no magic formulas. Most things do not come to us easily. Building relationships is a difficult process; it does not happen just because people share the same blood (family ties). No two people are alike — even in families. Unfortunately, today there are many families without interpersonal relationships and caring among their members.

Communication Is the Key

When we understand someone we are better able to meet his needs. In the context of such a caring relationship, we can even make requests of the other person and be his friend. Such understanding and caring cannot occur without active communication on a heart-to-heart level.

Modern life-styles seem to militate against such effectiveness in relationships. While parents are frequently busy building their careers and accounts, young people have more free time than ever. Such an abundance of leisure leads them in many directions. To fill their time (and perhaps a sense of emptiness), young people search for a variety of outlets. Partying, entertainment, "escapism," and materialism reflect the values of the age. The peer group reflects these values and a subtle pressure to conform becomes very influential.

The entertainment media focus on the youths of today because they realize their tremendous purchasing power. Consequently, much advertising and marketing is directed toward young people. The fashions, fads and fantasies portrayed on the screens of the media are translated into reality in the minds and life-styles of today's youths.

Inherited Irresponsibility

The 1960s were a decade of turbulence and shifting values. The quiet and relatively simple life-styles of the fifties' family were replaced by attitudes of rebellion toward all forms of authority — parents, religion, government, education, etc.

Adult responsibilities were reevaluated by the young who began with a desire to replace phony values with honest ones. The process went beyond this goal, however, and the result was an expansive, rebellious attitude.

The breakdown of the family (with half the marriages ending in divorce, single-parent families, latch-key children, children of divorce, sexual abuse, physical abuse, emotional abuse) left many people wandering in a blurry fog without values, purpose or a sense of responsibility.

The trend continues. Now children learn their value systems primarily from television and the public schools. Many families rarely have meals together. Communication between parents and children frequently takes the form of: "Can I have $5.00 for a movie?" "Sure, son," rather than honest, open sharing of feelings and concerns.

Overcoming Obstacles to Communication

How do we learn to communicate? As is true with all skills, communication has to be learned through practice. Essentially, it takes at least one person who is committed to working at it. Ideally, it takes two people who agree together to make it work.

Let's begin by identifying some of the obstacles to open, honest communication. In so doing, we can quickly see what is needed to make honest communication occur.

Advice to Parents

I'd like to speak to parents first. It is good to remember that children learn, first and foremost, from you. Your attitudes, values, opinions and behaviors form a model from which your children begin to pattern their lives.

Do you model all the values and behaviors you expect from your children? Being a parent in today's society requires all the love, commitment, wisdom and common sense any person can possibly muster with the help of God. Without Him, such a heavy responsibility seems impossible.

While the Bible tells children to "Obey your parents in the Lord" (Eph. 6:1), it also says, "Fathers, provoke not your children to wrath" (Eph 6:4). Perhaps nothing is quite so wrath-producing as the parental expectation, "Do as I say; not as I do."

The primary responsibility of a parent is to provide a consistent, caring example in front of his children. In so doing, a parent will assure that his children's role models will not come from the TV set, but rather from home, across the dinner table, at church and in society.

Every value and every underlying principle which a child will grow up with and later use to make difficult decisions comes from the parental figures of his childhood! A parent's absence (either physically or emotionally) will affect his child. Parents need to be there for their children. Irresponsibility in parenting always leads to problems in the lives of the children.

Advice to Teenagers

You are certainly going through a difficult time in your life. Fundamentally, however, you are the one who must begin accepting responsibility for your life.

If you are a Christian, you need to be sure you are upholding Jesus Christ without compromise in all that you do. His Lordship in your life should affect your choices in music, the clothes you wear, the words you say, the friends you select, the way you treat other people and the respect you give to your parents and other adults. God holds you accountable in all these areas of your life.

There is simply no justification for rebellion. Despite the way rebellion is sometime glorified in the media, there is little (if any) actual glory in it. Rebellion leads to drug abuse, suicide, sexual problems (including diseases), unwanted pregnancies, abortions, divorce and increasing crime rates.

Accepting Responsibility

When parents and teens accept their responsibilities to each other, good and lasting relationships can be built. Avoiding those responsibilities leads to failure.

The process of building a relationship begins with communication, is maintained by communication and thrives on communication.

When a mediator guides rival or enemy nations to a treaty, he leads them into an understanding of one another. The more they understand each other, the easier it will be for them to arrive at acceptable terms of agreement. Is it any wonder that there is so little agreement in families when the average family spends only four minutes a day talking to one another?

Both parents and young people need to keep in mind that communication is a two-way street. It involves both talking and listening (with the emphasis placed on listening — not just listening to the words but also for the feelings being expressed).

It is difficult for teens to understand statements such as: "You do it just because I said so." How can a young person relate to an explanation that begins, "In my day. . ."? Communication is not preaching and/or lecturing; neither is it yelling and screaming. First and foremost, it is *listening*.

Both parents and youths need to communicate more than their opinions, but also why they feel the way they do. The one basic assurance a parent should give to his child is: "I want you to know that you can talk to me about anything at anytime. I want to hear what you feel about things. I am concerned about the issues of your life."

In the same way, the young person needs to learn to listen for the feelings behind what their parents say and do. A good common rule to use is: Have mutual respect for each other. (This is also known as the Golden Rule, and it should govern all our relationships, especially the relationship between a parent and a child.)

On-the-job Training

Life does not come with a manual that specifically delineates the way to respond to every situation that comes up. (The Bible, of course, is the closest thing we have to such a manual.) The key is found in effort and commitment.

As we learn to keep our lives focused and centered on Jesus Christ, we learn how to communicate with others in our family and other spheres of our life. God has promised to give us the strength to work through all our problems, and the parent-teenager relationship is no exception to this.

In a home where openness, trust and sharing are encouraged, there are fewer problems. So many of the problems faced by young people today could be avoided if our families would follow the biblical values of family life and relationships.

16
CONCLUSION

There will come a time to every person when the most important thing in the universe will be his or her immortal soul. This will be a time when physical consciousness will cease and spiritual consciousness will begin. The decisions you make in this life, in the here and now, will determine the blessing and joy, or damnation and horror of your soul's eternity.

It is not necessary to choose Satan in order for your soul to exist eternally separated from God. All that is necessary is to not choose the Lord. Also, by choosing to do things God forbids, choices are made against God himself. Consulting an oracle — a demon — or looking to the stars or to the universe for advice instead of turning to God means you have made a choice against God.

Ouija Boards, Tarot cards, runes, crystals, astrology, and the other oracle-consulting methods or tools are not games. They were created and have been used to contact the dark side of the spiritual world. Their function has never changed. *They are not of God, and they are dangerous.*

Occultism is at an all-time peak. If it is not studied, understood, addressed and challenged, countless lives will be destroyed. I have witnessed the destructive force of satanism and the occult and for that reason it is difficult for me to remain coldly journalistic in my writing.

The New Age Movement is growing and more and more people are groping for new spiritual horizons. There is a growing belief that we are experiencing an evolutionary flux in religion in which old concepts of spirituality, born of ignorance, are passing away as new, more unconfining and knowledgeable concepts arise. Those who believe this should look more closely at the origins of these beliefs. *They are not new.*

In the past 100 years, new concepts have *not* arisen, rather, old, even ancient concepts have been reborn. The Ouija Board was rediscovered in 1891. Tarot cards resurfaced in the late 1800's, and did not become popular until the beginning of this century. Runecraft was all but forgotten until its strange rebirth in 1902.

The concepts behind all of the New Age beliefs are ancient and only became rearranged into the New Age package when Madame Blavatsky formed the Theosophical Society in 1875.

Astrology, almost killed by the science of astronomy, experienced its repopularization in the 1960's. The so-called modern religious beliefs of today are not a step forward, but are, indeed, a step back. The only revolutionary step man has ever made in religious beliefs happened nearly 2,000 years ago when Jesus Christ died on the cross and rose from the dead.

His light shone in the darkness, but the darkness could not comprehend it. The same is true today. The light of Jesus Christ shines in the darkness, but the darkness cannot receive it.

Jesus is the light, the true Light, "Which lighteth every man that cometh into the world" (John 1:9).

"He came unto his own, and his own received him not. But as many as received him, to them gave he power to become the sons of God, even to them that believe on his name" (John 1:11-12).

This wonderful power can be yours. Have you believed on the name of Jesus Christ? St. Paul wrote, "That if thou shalt confess with thy mouth the Lord Jesus, and shalt believe in thine heart that God hath raised him from the dead, thou shalt be saved" (Rom. 10:9).

If you would like to receive Jesus Christ as your Savior and Lord, please pray with me the following confession:

Lord, I recognize my need for you. By an act of faith and a choice of my will, I am making a decision to follow Jesus for the rest of my life. Without Him I am nothing. I have sinned and fallen far short of your glory.

I repent of my sins, Lord Jesus. Thank you for being a sacrifice for my sins. Thank you for loving me and dying for me. I receive you into my heart and life, and I ask you to guide me and direct me from this point forward.

I believe in you with all my heart. Fill
me with your Spirit. You died to set me free
from my sins. Thank you, Lord.

Welcome into the family of God. You have
decided to join the one group of people on earth who
know how to beat the odds, exemplify excellence,
and effect true, lasting changes in the lives of
others.

God has led me into a ministry known as
Radical Teens for Christ. If we can be of service to
you, please write to:

Radical Teens for Christ
P.O. Box 372
McAlester, OK 74502

Please remember, I will be praying for you.
God loves you, and He will never let you down!

— Sean Sellers

APPENDIX

Christian books for further study on Astrology:

1. Bullinger, E.W., *Witness of the Stars,* Grand Rapids, Michigan; Kregel, 1893, 1967.

2. Carr-Harris, Bertha. *The Heiroglyphics of the Heavens,* Toronto, Armac Press, 1933.

3. Flemming, Kenneth C., *God's Voice in the Stars: Zodiac Signs and Bible Truth,* Neptune, New Jersey, 1927, 1981.

4. Morris, Henry M., *Many Infallible Proofs,* San Diego, California: Creation Life Publishers, 1974.

5. Rolleston, Frances. *Mazzaroth or the Constellations,* Keswick, England, 1863.

6. Seiss, Joseph A., *The Gospel in the Stars,* Castel Press, 1884, Grand Rapids, Michigan: Kregel, 1979.

7. Spenser, Duane E., *Mazzaroth.* San Antonio, Texas: Word of Grace, 1972.